# Cue-Centered Therapy for Youth Experiencing Posttraumatic Symptoms

PROGRAMS THAT WORK

# Cue-Centered Therapy for Youth Experiencing Posttraumatic Symptoms

## A Structured, Multimodal Intervention

THERAPIST GUIDE

VICTOR G. CARRIÓN

OXFORD
UNIVERSITY PRESS

OXFORD
UNIVERSITY PRESS

Oxford University Press is a department of the University of Oxford. It furthers the University's objective of excellence in research, scholarship, and education by publishing worldwide.

Oxford New York
Auckland Cape Town Dar es Salaam Hong Kong Karachi
Kuala Lumpur Madrid Melbourne Mexico City Nairobi
New Delhi Shanghai Taipei Toronto

With offices in
Argentina Austria Brazil Chile Czech Republic France Greece
Guatemala Hungary Italy Japan Poland Portugal Singapore
South Korea Switzerland Thailand Turkey Ukraine Vietnam

Oxford is a registered trademark of Oxford University Press in the UK and certain other countries.

Published in the United States of America by
Oxford University Press
198 Madison Avenue, New York, NY 10016



Library of Congress Cataloging-in-Publication Data
Names: Carrion, Victor G.
Title: Cue-centered therapy for youth experiencing posttraumatic symptoms : a structured multimodal intervention, therapist guide / Victor G. Carrión.
Description: Oxford ; New York : Oxford University Press, [2016] | Series: Programs that work | Includes bibliographical references.
Identifiers: LCCN 2015036626 | ISBN 9780190201326 (paperback)
Subjects: LCSH: Post-traumatic stress disorder in children—Treatment. | Therapist and patient. | Families. | BISAC: PSYCHOLOGY / Clinical Psychology.
Classification: LCC RJ506.P55 C37 2016 | DDC 618.92/8521—dc23 LC record available at http://lccn.loc.gov/2015036626

Mahatma Ghandi accurately stated, “Poverty is the worst form of violence.” To this I humbly add, “Lack of education is the worst type of traumatic insult.” This book is intended to empower through knowledge.

This book is dedicated to my mother, Sra. Sylvia Rodriguez, who taught me the value of resilience.

# About PROGRAMS THAT WORK

Stunning developments in healthcare have taken place over the last several years, but many of our widely accepted interventions and strategies in mental health and behavioral medicine have been brought into question by research evidence as not only lacking benefit, but perhaps, inducing harm (Barlow, 2010). Other strategies have been proven effective using the best current standards of evidence, resulting in broad-based recommendations to make these practices more available to the public (McHugh & Barlow, 2010). Several recent developments are behind this revolution. First, we have arrived at a much deeper understanding of pathology, both psychological and physical, which has led to the development of new, more precisely targeted interventions. Second, our research methodologies have improved substantially, such that we have reduced threats to internal and external validity, making the outcomes more directly applicable to clinical situations. Third, governments around the world and healthcare systems and policymakers have decided that the quality of care should improve, that it should be evidence based, and that it is in the public's interest to ensure that this happens (Barlow, 2004; Institute of Medicine, 2001; McHugh & Barlow, 2010).

Of course, the major stumbling block for clinicians everywhere is the accessibility of newly developed evidence-based psychological interventions. Workshops and books can go only so far in acquainting responsible and conscientious practitioners with the latest behavioral healthcare practices and their applicability to individual patients. This new series, Programs *ThatWork*™, is devoted to communicating these exciting new interventions to clinicians on the frontlines of practice.

The manuals and workbooks in this series contain step-by-step detailed procedures for assessing and treating specific problems and diagnoses. But this series also goes beyond the books and manuals by providing ancillary materials that will approximate the supervisory process in assisting practitioners in the implementation of these procedures in their practice.

In our emerging healthcare system, the growing consensus is that evidence-based practice offers the most responsible course of action for the mental health professional. All behavioral healthcare clinicians deeply desire to provide the best possible care for their patients. In this series, our aim is to close the dissemination and information gap and make that possible.

This manual offers guidance to therapists treating the complex clinical scenarios of chronically traumatized children. A traumatic event can result in negative mental and physical health effects, and childhood trauma can be particularly detrimental. It can lead to PTSD, anxiety disorders, depression, dissociation, externalizing behavioral problems, and suicidal ideation, and trauma has been associated with attentional impairment, cognitive performance, and the development of self-regulation.

Cue-Centered Therapy (CCT), described in this Therapist Guide, utilizes a hybrid of interventions shown to be effective in treating trauma and was designed to address the four core domains of cognition, emotion, physiology, and behavior. While the therapist facilitates the therapy as teacher and collaborator, CCT also calls for the child to actively participate in every aspect of her treatment, which emphasizes the importance of empowering the child through knowledge to become her own agent of change. Rather than having the child attempt to "unlearn" maladaptive responses to traumatic reminders, CCT focuses on facilitating development of more adaptive responses in each of the four domains. This structured and flexible guide is appropriate for use with children eight years of age or older and can be administered by mental health professionals in a variety of settings including outpatient clinics, community mental health centers, and schools.

Anne Marie Albano, Editor-in-Chief
David H. Barlow, Editor-in-Chief
Programs *ThatWork*

## References


Barlow, D.H. (2004). Psychological treatments. *American Psychologist, 59*, 869-878.

Barlow, D.H. (2010). Negative effects from psychological treatments: A perspective. *American Psychologist, 65(2)*, 13-20.

Institute of Medicine. (2001). Crossing the quality chasm: *A new health system for the 21st century.* Washington, DC: National Academy Press.

McHugh, R.K., & Barlow, D.H. (2010). Dissemination and implementation of evidence-based psychological interventions: A review of current efforts. *American Psychologist, 65(2)*, 73-84.

# Contents

## Phase 4

# Acknowledgments

I thank the families and children who inspired this book and the many clinicians who offered their advice, contributed feedback, and read early drafts: Laura Strom, Katherine Hull, Lynda Heiden, Alicia Lieberman, Judith Cohen, John Rettger, Stephanie Evans, and Cynthia Kane-Hyman.

Special thanks to Hilit Kletter who informed clinical input through practice and helped formulate key concepts. Thanks to Alex Basile in helping with the final drafts. I am also appreciative of my colleagues in Spain, Prudencio Rodriguez and Paz Quijano, who provided feedback on cultural adaptations.

I thank the Lucile Packard Foundation for Children's Health and, in particular Dana Pace and Rachel Olinger, and the anonymous donors whose support made this work possible, including the development, evaluation, and dissemination of cue-centered therapy.

Last, I thank my family and my partner, John Ashworth, for their support, patience, and guidance.

# Cue-Centered Therapy for Youth Experiencing Posttraumatic Symptoms

# CHAPTER 1 Introductory Information for Therapists

## Background Information and Purpose of Cue-Centered Therapy

Cue-centered therapy (CCT) is appropriate for use with youths age 8 years or older who have been exposed to chronic traumatic experiences, who may continue to experience traumatic events during the course of treatment, or who are at risk of recurrence of trauma after treatment. Although CCT aims primarily to treat posttraumatic stress symptoms, associated symptoms of depression and anxiety are also addressed. CCT may be used to treat a wide range of traumas, including physical and sexual abuse, the witnessing of violence, and experiencing natural or man-made disasters. CCT can be administered by mental health professionals in a variety of settings, such as outpatient clinics, community mental health centers, and schools.

Fundamental to the therapy described in this manual is the principle that trauma exposure can result in an interactive variety of cognitive, emotional, physiological, and behavioral symptoms. Reexposure to traumatic reminders, or cues, can cause exacerbation of these symptoms. Through a combination of empirically supported interventions and CCT-specific interventions, CCT is designed to address the four core domains of cognition, emotion, physiology, and behavior.

CCT has several unique components that set it apart from other standard interventions. The child participates actively in every aspect of CCT treatment, whereas the therapist facilitates as a teacher and collaborator. Rather than receiving a passive, static intervention, the child propels session-to-session progress actively by identifying relevant cues, giving updates on progress to caregivers, and developing coping tools. The therapy focuses on helping youths develop insight into their own histories and current patterns of behavior and emotion. CCT derives its name from its focus on the conditioning process that results in sensitivity toward trauma-related cues. Rather than having youths attempt to "unlearn" maladaptive responses conditioned to cues, CCT focuses on creating new connections and behavioral responses.

Although CCT focuses primarily on individual therapy with the child, it is still essential for the therapist to develop a strong relationship with the caregivers early during treatment. Acknowledging that many caregivers cannot attend sessions at either the school or the clinic because of other life-sustaining obligations, a minimal number of four sessions require the participation of the caregiver. These sessions have been selected carefully—assessment, psychoeducation, midtherapy update, and one of the closing sessions—to help facilitate caregivers' coaching and support.

CCT's combination of insight and cognitive, behavioral, expressive, psychoeducational, and family approaches aims to target the four core domains of a response: thought, emotion, physiology, and behavior. The therapy is designed to reduce negative cognitions, foster emotional expression, identify and change trauma-related responses, empower youths, and strengthen the relationship between caregivers and their children. Through CCT, youths and their caregivers learn to recognize and manage maladaptive responses effectively that occur when exposed to traumatic reminders. Evaluating the reactions in the four domains facilitates the development of more adaptive responses.

## Manual Structure

This manual consists of a session-by-session breakdown of CCT (see "Outline of This Treatment Program" later in this chapter). Each session presents materials needed, a session outline, and a session overview that details goals and the therapist's role, followed by step-by-step instructions for that session. After each session, a review form is provided and is to be used as a checklist for the therapist for the objectives for that particular session. It also encourages annotating progress notes. Illustrations, figures, or forms shared with the child or caregivers are also included at the end of each session chapter, and may be photocopied for use with clients.

### Use of Terms

This manual switches between using *he/him* and *she/her* to refer to both girls and boys in treatment. *Children* and *youths* are the terms used for children and adolescents. *Caregiver* implies one or more caregivers. Italics are used to indicate clinical scenarios and to provide sample scripts.

## Disorder or Problem Focus

### Understanding Trauma

Therapists, counselors, and other professionals who work with children are exposed to vivid accounts of trauma as experienced by children and their families. The National Institute of Mental Health (NIMH) (2013) defines psychological trauma as an emotionally painful, shocking, distressing, or even life-threatening experience that can result in negative mental and physical health effects. The impact of trauma may be intensified by a variety of factors, creating a particularly significant insult on the body during development.

Children may experience a broad range of traumatic events, ranging from large-scale (e.g., community violence, natural catastrophes) to interpersonal (e.g., physical abuse, sexual abuse, witnessing violence) trauma, to traumatic losses or separations (e.g., the death of a loved one, being kidnapped). Trauma exposure in childhood can result in a variety of psychological symptoms, including posttraumatic stress disorder (PTSD), other stress and anxiety disorders, depression, dissociation, externalizing behavioral problems, and suicidal ideation (Abram et al., 2004; Kilpatrick et al., 2003; Lansford et al., 2002; Lewis et al., 2012).

Trauma may also result in substance use, school disengagement, and academic difficulties (Anda et al., 2006; Cooley-Strickland et al., 2009). Certain behaviors may be associated with certain types of abuse. For example, adolescents with a history of physical abuse are more likely to smoke cigarettes, use cocaine, and engage in risky sexual behaviors compared with adolescents with no history of physical abuse (Rodgers et al., 2004). Trauma is also associated with poor attentional skills, cognitive difficulties, and reduced self-regulation of emotion (Cooley-Strickland et al., 2009; Donnelly & Amaya-Jackson, 2002). The absence of literature findings on childhood granting resilience supports the opposite notion: sensitive physiological systems go through critical periods of development during which disruptions can lead to long-term neurological and psychological consequences.

Experiencing trauma during childhood and adolescence can have far-reaching public health consequences. In 2008, The National Survey of Children's Exposure to Violence sampled 4,569 children aged 0 to 17 years and found that more than 55% had experienced a physical assault, 8% had been sexually assaulted, and 9% had been assaulted with a weapon (Finkelhor, Turner, Ormrod, & Hamby, 2010). The rates are greater for adolescents, who generally experience more sexual assaults and witness more community violence (Finkelhor et al., 2010). Prevalence studies indicate that 38% of adolescents are exposed to community violence and 9% are exposed to parental violence (Lewis et al., 2012). In one nationally representative sample of 2,000 children aged 10 to 16 years, more than 40% of youths reported at least one traumatic experience (Costello, Erkanli, Fairbank, & Angold, 2002).

Although these high rates reflect more sensitive recognition of child abuse and other forms of trauma during the past 10 years, certain types of abuse or trauma may be occurring with greater frequency. Issues such as unemployment and economic decline can increase the rates of child abuse and trauma. Because cumulative exposure to violence poses significant problems for children and adolescents—including anxiety, depression, and aggressive behavior—developing interventions for these children is critical. Widom and colleagues found that exposure to one traumatic event increases the likelihood of revictimization (Widom, Czaja, & Dutton, 2008). Children who experience multiple traumatic events in the face of adversity need treatments tailored to their experience, one that is often complicated by community violence, multiple home placements, grief, loss of caregivers, and other events (Many, 2009).

Physical and emotional neglect is the most common type of abuse. Childhood neglect accounts for about 59% of cases reported to Child Protective Services in the United States and has links to poor outcomes later in life (Nikulina, Widom, & Czaja, 2011). A child who experiences neglect may have different symptoms than a child who is exposed to community violence, and these two may differ from a third who sustains both neglect and violence. They may also share symptoms. On the other hand, even when two children experience the same type of trauma, they may develop significantly different symptoms. The unique emotional, behavioral, and biological outcome of trauma results from complex individual and universal equations that include biological and environmental variables.

### Understanding PTSD Symptoms

PTSD first appeared in the *Diagnostic and Statistical Manual for Mental Disorders* (DSM) in 1980. Most of the research on PTSD at the time was conducted on male combat veterans. Being sensitive to the different developmental manifestations of these symptoms in children, researchers and clinicians modified descriptions in subsequent revisions of the DSM.

The lifetime prevalence rate for PTSD is reported to be approximately 7% for the adult American population (Kessler et al., 2005). The estimated lifetime prevalence rate of PTSD in the general adolescent population is between 2% and 8%, with greater rates for girls than boys (Abram et al., 2004; Merikangas et al., 2010). When we recruited children who witnessed interpersonal violence, we reported a full diagnosis of PTSD in 57.5% of the sample (Kletter, Weems, & Carrion, 2009). Other investigators have reported similar rates in children who experience multiple traumatic events (Cisler et al., 2012; Copeland, Keeler, Angold, & Costello, 2007). The number of traumatic experiences in a lifetime also predicts severity of PTSD, as well as severity of anxiety, depression, and dissociation (Briere, Kaltman, & Green, 2008; Rodgers et al., 2004).

Rates of PTSD are also elevated—in the range of 10% to 50%, for many children with a single traumatic event. These prevalence rates might be even greater if subsyndromal posttraumatic symptoms are taken into account (Cuffe et al., 1998). Youth experiencing subthreshold posttraumatic symptoms do not differ significantly from youths who meet full PTSD criteria in terms of impairment and distress (Carrion, Weems, Ray, & Reiss, 2002b). As most clinicians can attest, a child does not need a diagnosis of PTSD to experience significant social, emotional, and academic difficulties. These children without a diagnosis of PTSD, and at times without any other diagnosis, have symptoms that still warrant treatment.

The prevalence of child and adolescent traumatization and PTSD in clinical or legal settings is even more striking. Among children and adolescents seeking treatment in clinical outpatient settings, between 60% and 90% have been exposed to trauma (Schneider, Grilli, & Schneider, 2013). Among a sample of 36 young adults with psychotic symptoms aged 15 to 25 years, 64% reported a history of childhood trauma and

39% reported PTSD symptoms as a result of childhood trauma (Bendall, Alvarez-Jimenez, Hulbert, McGorry, & Jackson, 2012). Abram and colleagues interviewed 892 juvenile detainees and identified trauma in 90% of the sample, with a mean of approximately 14 traumatic experiences (Abram et al., 2004). Between 51% and 82% of court-referred adolescents and juvenile delinquents report having experienced trauma, many of whom display symptoms of PTSD and dissociation (Brosky & Lally, 2004; Plattner et al., 2003).

Most children with PTSD exhibit symptoms of other conditions as well. Although these indicators may reflect a distinct disorder, they could also reflect symptom overlap among conditions, including anxiety, depression, attention-deficit hyperactivity disorder (ADHD), oppositional defiant disorder, and dissociative disorders (Murphy, Rosen, Cameron, & Thompson, 2002; Terranova, Boxer, & Morris, 2009). Associated problems include truancy and school suspension, social withdrawal, aggressive and delinquent behavior, substance use and abuse, thought disorders, emotional dysregulation, poor physical health, suicidal thoughts, and suicide attempts (Abram et al., 2007; Anda et al., 2006; Bendall et al., 2012; Cisler et al., 2012; Kilpatrick et al., 2003; Lewis et al., 2012; Terranova et al., 2009). A large survey of more than 4,000 adolescents found that 8% of the adolescents who experienced a traumatic event in the previous 6 months met criteria for PTSD and 15% met criteria for a major depressive episode (Hansen et al., 2008).

The long-lasting effects of childhood trauma lead to adult depression and anxiety. A greater number of traumatic events in childhood will produce greater symptoms in adulthood (Chu, William, Harris, Bryant, & Gatt, 2013). One study of more than 2,000 female university students found a linear relationship between the number of childhood traumas and symptoms in adulthood (Briere et al., 2008). Some adult health risk behaviors (such as smoking, obesity, numerous sexual partners, and a sedentary lifestyle) and associated medical diseases (such as sexually transmitted diseases, cancer, diabetes, cardiac disease, and chronic bronchitis and emphysema) have been shown to occur more often in adults abused as children (Anda et al., 2006; Rodgers et al., 2004). Higher rates of eating disorders, antisocial behavior, and personality disorders have also been found in adults that experienced childhood trauma (Rodgers et al., 2004).

## How This Manual Came To Be

Nearly 10 years ago, as I was recruiting participants for my neuroimaging and endocrinology studies of pediatric PTSD, I came to a startling realization; many children with stressful lives who were attending clinics for behavioral, emotional, or academic problems were not receiving appropriate treatment for their presenting issues. Although caregivers were surprised to learn that children can develop posttraumatic symptoms, children were under the impression they were receiving treatment because they were bad, delinquent, or crazy. Therapists were overwhelmed, burdened by the adversities their families faced and challenged by the lack of response to treatment. Many of the therapists felt adrift in their treatment, without a clear focus or collective agenda. Yet, there was in all of them—caregivers, children, and therapists—a desire to learn more, a conviction that more could be done, and an extraordinary will to participate in any studies that would provide them with more knowledge about trauma and its effects.

It became evident that effective treatments were compromised by a number of factors; caregivers were not engaging in treatment as often as their therapist would have liked, children had difficulty describing circumscribed events on which to anchor their treatment, and therapists were confronting ongoing events in the lives of their clients that disrupted the progress of therapy. All these factors led to a team that felt discouraged and helpless, even if well intentioned. I wondered how this could be possible when protocols had been developed that offered guidelines, approaches, and training for the treatment of trauma in children. As I traveled to present and discuss my biological research findings at other centers, I continued to hear the same plea: "We need something to treat these kids."

My response was guided by the fact that these were not kids who had experienced discreet traumas in their distant pasts, but who continued to experience traumatic stress and adversity throughout their development. These were not kids to whom something bad had happened last week or last year, but for whom exposure to domestic and community violence, lack of school resources, poor nutrition, parental unemployment, housing insecurity, grief, hunger, and loss had become intermingled with other traumatic events in a knot of stressors that comprised the bulk of their young lives.

Working with these children illuminated a startling synergy between events: more adversity increases the risk of experiencing additional adversity. The fact that traumatic events become a way of life for many children can hardly soften the blow of their stories or the effects of the trauma. The physiological changes associated with threat and fear are still present. In fact, they become more harmful in individuals with increased frequency of exposure. An effective treatment would need to be focused, tailored to the child's experience, and flexible, bringing different modalities to the therapist's armamentarium.

The primary obstacle to the delivery of this treatment is avoidance, or the failure to address a traumatic experience. Characteristically insidious, inconspicuous, and pervasive, avoidance can be found throughout society—in families, clinics, schools, and in the media. Many of us would rather look away from a tragedy, particularly one involving children, than confront it. Yet it is that exact response on which PTSD thrives. The longer a trauma is ignored, the stronger its effects become. The antithesis to avoidance is approach. Stanford psychiatrist David Spiegel once told me, "When someone breaks an arm and goes to the emergency room, to treat the arm you have to touch it and it's going to hurt, but it's the only way in which the arm will recover." We need to approach the problem and probe it to begin the healing process.

To plan therapy with a single approach is like performing surgery with only a scalpel. In the same way that surgeons benefit from using retractors, scissors, and forceps, and other equipment, the astute therapist can also benefit from a wide range of tools and techniques. Yet, although child psychotherapy has made tremendous strides toward understanding and combining diverse cognitive and behavioral strategies, the structuring of insight-oriented techniques has received little attention compared with others. Insight, the ability to gain knowledge from one's experience, helps children make sense of their past; their feelings of fear, sadness, and anger; and their current maladaptive behaviors or symptoms. Gaining insight empowers children through knowledge and increases self-reliance when supportive resources are scarce.

It is imperative to educate children and caregivers about trauma and its effects in a clear, direct, and hopeful way. Communication to teachers, health providers, case workers, and other caregivers is vital to deliver a consistent message and to avoid misguided attitudes and approaches. Education and communication are examples of approaching the problem rather than avoiding it. It is essential to communicate that treatments are available, effective, and beneficial when we adhere to existing protocols.

The effects of such complicated traumatic histories, however, cannot be undone with an isolated therapeutic experience. Real progress requires the ongoing practice of skills learned throughout an intervention. Children need to be equipped with knowledge that will help them face and overcome ongoing and future traumatic events. Thus, our response to the caregivers' plea is a structured approach to treatment that captures the child's full life experience, fosters the development of insight, and guides the therapist with clear objectives on what needs to be accomplished. The resulting product is the 15-session intervention called *cue-centered therapy*.

## CCT: Evidence-Based Treatment

CCT incorporates evidence-based treatments for childhood trauma and educates children on how to become their own agents of change. CCT increases the child's understanding of a traumatic experience and its associated symptoms, as well as provides effective methods to counteract them. By increasing a child's insight into the relationship among trauma history, current emotions, and behavioral responses, CCT enables the child to learn how they relate to subconscious trauma-related cues that were not accessible previously.

The elements described in this manual are considered important for treatment success. They have been studied carefully in a randomized controlled trial (Carrion, Kletter, Weems, Berry, & Rettger, 2013) in which children with a history of interpersonal violence were randomized into a CCT group or a waitlist control group. Youths were considered appropriate for the study if they were between 8 years and 17 years old, had a history of exposure to violence, had a nonabusing caretaker willing to participate in the study, and had no current exposure to perpetrators of violence. Two licensed therapists (one with a doctorate in psychology [PhD] and one with a masters in family therapy [MFT]) with experience in the treatment of childhood trauma were trained for 3 months in administrating the CCT protocol. The therapists also had weekly supervision, phone consultations, and case conferences. Fidelity to the treatment protocol (which was determined to be 91.2%) was assessed by two independent research assistants who used a fidelity form.

Youths were excluded from the study if they had significant medical illness, documentation of a diagnosis of autism or schizophrenia, history of mental retardation or an intelligence quotient (IQ) less than 70, substance dependency, or lack of proficiency in English. The final sample consisted of 65 youths who were assigned randomly by the study coordinator either to CCT treatment ($n$ = 38) or to a waitlist control group ($n$ = 27) and to one of two therapists using a computer-generated number series. All participants reported exposure to at least two traumatic events; the most common traumas reported included separation/loss (75.0%), witnessing violence (61.5%), homicide (51.9%), and being subjected to physical abuse (25.0%) and bullying (25.0%). No significant differences were found between the waitlist and treatment groups regarding the amount of violence exposure ($t$[59] = 0.801, $p$ = .426).

After treatment, individuals who received the intervention had fewer posttraumatic symptoms, as measured by PTSD Reaction Index (PTSD-RI) scores, than those in the waitlist group ($t$[41] = 3.10, $p$ = .004). Analysis of PTSD-RI scores indicated there was a significant effect for treatment group in both the linear ($t$[96] = –2.17, $p$ = .033) and quadratic ($t$[96] = 2.02, $p$ = .046) analyses, suggesting greater and faster symptom reductions in the treatment group. Using hierarchical linear model analyses, Carrion and colleagues examined self-reported anxiety with the Revised Children's Manifest Anxiety Scale and evaluated depression with the Children's Depression Inventory (Carrion et al., 2013). Results indicated significant linear ($t$[90] = –3.21, $p$ = .002) and quadratic ($t$[90] = 2.29, $p$ = .025) effects on level 1 for anxiety, and a linear trend for depression ($t$[93] = 1.78, $p$ = .078). Follow-up indicated a much larger reduction in parent-reported posttraumatic-symptoms scores (PTSD-RI–Parent Version) from pre- to posttreatment in the intervention group, and little or no change in the waitlisted group. Follow-up indicated a reduction in Beck's Anxiety Inventory scores for caregivers from pre- to posttreatment during the intervention, and an increase in anxiety for the caregivers on the waitlist group. There was a significant decrease of PTSD symptoms across sessions. In addition, treatment maintenance was examined using a series of paired sample $t$-tests comparing posttreatment symptoms with symptoms reported at follow-up. There were no significant differences between posttreatment and the 3-month follow-up for self-reported posttraumatic symptoms ($t$[36] = –1.15, $p$ = .259); however, there was a significant decrease in posttraumatic symptoms as scored by the caregivers ($t[34] = 3.78, p = .001$), suggesting continued improvement from the perspective of the caregiver.

The study provided preliminary evidence of the feasibility and efficacy of CCT for reducing posttraumatic stress and anxiety in children exposed to ongoing violence. CCT was also associated with improvement in youths' overall functioning as rated by the therapists, who used the Children's Global Assessment Scale. Furthermore, treatment gains were maintained over time. As symptoms decreased, functioning improved across time. These results demonstrate that, compared with the waitlist group, the CCT group had greater reductions in PTSD symptoms by both caregiver and self-reports (Carrion et al., 2013).

## Therapy Technique: A Hybrid of Empirically Validated Modalities

### Cognitive–Behavioral Therapy

Research suggests that cognitive–behavioral therapy (CBT) may be the treatment of choice for traumatized youths because it has significant empirical support. Several controlled studies of cognitive–behavioral treatment have demonstrated reductions in children's PTSD symptomatology, depression, and anxiety after treatment (Smith et al., 2013). Studies comparing children treated with CBT with those receiving other or no treatments have demonstrated the positive therapeutic effects of CBT on PTSD, behavioral problems, anxiety, and depression. These effects have been demonstrated to continue after treatment (Schneider et al., 2013).

In a meta-analysis, Silverman and colleagues (2008) found that CBT interventions were more successful in reducing PTSD symptoms, depression, and behavioral problems than non-CBT interventions. A randomized controlled study comparing trauma-focused cognitive–behavioral therapy (TF-CBT) and child-centered interventions for sexually abused youths and adolescents found that TF-CBT resulted in significantly fewer PTSD symptoms, behavioral problems, and abuse-related attributions, and less depression and shame in trauma survivors (Cohen, Deblinger, Mannarino, & Steer, 2004). Caregivers involved in TF-CBT also had significantly less depression and distress, and showed significantly more support and effective parenting toward their children after treatment than parents in the child-centered condition (Cohen et al., 2004).

### Exposure

The behavioral technique of exposure to the trauma narrative and traumatic reminders has been applied in several studies. In one randomized control trial comparing prolonged exposure with psychodynamic therapy for adolescents with PTSD, the prolonged exposure group experienced a more significant reduction in PTSD and depressive symptoms as well as reduced symptomology at the 6-month follow-up (Smith et al., 2013). Exposure helps to disrupt the association between ongoing feelings of fear and the traumatic reminders (Silva et al., 2003). Over time, exposure techniques can decrease trauma-related avoidance and fear through the process of extinction (Cohen et al., 2000). The mental link between the trauma and the ongoing sense of fear and threat can be weakened, and the trauma can be placed in the past rather than the present (Silva et al., 2003).

Child trauma studies have used various forms of exposure, including imaginal flooding, gradual exposure (Feeny, Foa, Treadwell, & March, 2004; Scheeringa et al., 2011; Silverman et al., 2008), and systematic desensitization (March, Amaya-Jackson, Murray, & Schulte, 1998). With gradual exposure, trauma cues and fear are unpaired through the process of habituation. The patient comes to tolerate the physical and physiological symptoms of anxiety and, eventually, no longer experiences the anxiety when presented with trauma reminders (Cohen, Mannarino, & Murray, 2011b; Dorsey, Briggs, & Woods, 2011).

Because trauma memories are often stored as sensations and feelings rather than as verbal narratives, it can be difficult for survivors to express their traumatic experiences verbally (Brewin & Saunders, 2001). Verbalization may be particularly difficult for children because of limited vocabulary or concrete thinking. Child studies often allow for children to explore the trauma through imagery, play, and art, but generally have the ultimate goal of helping the patient verbalize the trauma (Cohen & Mannarino, 2008; Scheeringa, Zeanah, & Cohen, 2010).

The telling of the trauma narrative is a form of imaginal exposure known as *narrative exposure* or *narrative storytelling.* Narrative exposure can help organize fragmented sensory and emotional memories, integrating them with autobiographical memory at the conscious, verbal level (Cohen et al., 2012; Silva et al., 2003). The trauma narrative can also serve to identify the cognitive distortions and misattributions that survivors may develop subsequent to trauma (Cohen & Mannarino, 2008; Cohen et al., 2012;

Silva et al., 2003). It has been suggested that involving caregivers in constructing the narrative can foster a better understanding of the role the trauma has played within the family (Schneider et al., 2013).

As a result of the trauma cue sensitivity experienced by survivors, many therapies include a cue exposure component in addition to narrative exposure. The trauma narrative has been used as a starting point to help address feared stimuli (Grasso, Joselow, Marquez, & Webb, 2011). When cues are identified, they can be confronted incrementally based on the youth's distress level (Cohen et al., 2012). These cues can be approached gradually, beginning with imaginal exposure and role-plays within therapy, and progressing to in vivo take-home assignments.

### Relaxation and Cognitive Coping Skills Training

Exposure can also be paired with relaxation and cognitive coping skills training (Cohen, Mannarino, Kliethermes, & Murray, 2012; Deblinger, Stauffer, & Steer, 2001; Scheeringa et al., 2010). Some therapists use relaxation training components, including progressive muscle relaxation, yoga, and dance (Cohen et al., 2012), as well as cognitive tools such as the Fear Thermometer and the Traffic Light (King et al., 2000; Silva et al., 2003; Wagner, 2002). In their use of TF-CBT with youth, Cohen and colleagues (2012) included case examples of youths using their own coping strategies, such as listening to music or watching television, as well as therapist-directed tools. The identification and development of coping skills tailored to the individual child has also been suggested by others as an effective method when working with this population (Silva et al., 2003).

The combination of exposure and cognitive restructuring techniques in trauma therapy enables the process of transforming traumatic memories from the sensory system to the verbal memory system. Through overcoming the pathological posttraumatic avoidance symptoms and processing the trauma consciously and verbally, intrusive emotional and physiological posttraumatic symptoms may also improve. This process involves elaborating memories and integrating them into a coherent view of the self and the world (Ehlers & Clark, 2000). The continual retelling of the trauma through narrative exposure leads both to symptom reduction and cognitive change (Cohen et al., 2011a; Silva et al., 2000). With each retelling, the narrative should become less affective, less sensory, and more verbal (Silva et al., 2000).

The relaxation and cognitive tools learned during therapy can be helpful in a child's everyday life, but they are also helpful during the therapeutic process; hence, these skills should be taught early during therapy. These skills help children experience more control over their feelings and provide a means to tolerate physiological hyperarousal or the reexperiencing symptoms (Cohen, 1998; Cohen, Perel, DeBellis, Friedman, & Putnam, 2002).

### Art, Play, and Movement Modalities

Art, play, and movement modalities have been used in other child trauma therapies as a way of ensuring rest and promoting expression (Chemtob, Nakashima, & Hamada, 2002b; Cohen et al., 2004; King et al., 2000). It has been suggested that aerobic exercise may help facilitate cognitive acceptance of physiological arousal and relief from posttraumatic symptoms (Newman & Motta, 2007).

### Cognitive Restructuring and Processing

Repeated cue exposure in therapy allows trauma survivors to work through cognitive distortions such as self-blame and guilt, and move toward more positive attributions (Bower & Sivers, 1998). More direct cognitive restructuring techniques can be included in therapy along with exposure (Feeny et al., 2004; King et al., 2000). This process involves identifying youths' current cognitions and their basis, and replacing them with more accurate attributions (Cohen et al., 2000).

Cognitive processing therapy, a form of CBT developed originally to treat adult sexual assault victims (House, 2006), has also been modified for use with child trauma survivors (Silverman et al., 2008). This therapy attempts to help trauma survivors change the trauma's meaning and to learn to assign appropriate meaning to both the trauma and their ongoing lives (Cohen et al., 2002). This is accomplished through extinction of intense negative emotions by exposing the patient to memories of the trauma (House, 2006). Cognitive processing therapy also aims to change cognitive distortions and maladaptive beliefs, particularly in the areas of safety, trust, control, and self-esteem (House, 2006). Reprocessing the trauma may help clarify distortions and misattributions. Different techniques to facilitate this reprocessing may include assertiveness training (House, 2006) and self-efficacy development (Dorsey et al., 2011).

### Psychoeducation

Education on the psychological factors related to the presenting problem for both trauma survivors and their parents has demonstrated effectiveness in outcomes (Scheeringa et al., 2010; Silverman et al., 2008). Because of the impact familial support and functioning can have on children's posttraumatic reactions and improvement in therapy, parental involvement in treatment is considered one of the integral components of child trauma treatment (Schneider et al., 2013). Psychoeducation promotes parental involvement. Parents and caregivers can play several important roles in child trauma treatment, helping to give their child a sense of safety and support, and helping the child resume activities abandoned after trauma (Silverman et al., 2008). Parental participation in treatment reduces dropout rates, reinforces therapeutic technique practice between sessions, and maintains clinical gains after treatment ends (Cohen et al., 2011a; Schneider et al., 2013).

In communities of poverty, with high rates of violence and scarce resources, however, it becomes difficult for many caregivers to engage in their child's treatment. The inability to miss work, the lack of childcare, and limited transportation are some of the factors that may interfere with parent engagement. Although their involvement must always be encouraged, other approaches are needed when caregivers are unavailable. Increased psychoeducation may be particularly helpful for children who are motivated for treatment and are psychologically minded (i.e., able to engage in conversations about feelings and emotions). The therapist must maximize psychoeducation with caregivers when they are available.

Providing children with psychoeducation about their condition and the treatment process is not only a sensible approach, but an ethical practice. Psychoeducation allows children to understand there are reasons behind their behaviors and symptoms. Parent and child education programs have been tested as key components in several different efficacious treatment programs for traumatized children (Deblinger, Stauffer, & Steer, 2001; King et al., 2000). Prior studies have included educational components such as providing a treatment rationale (Cohen & Mannarino, 2008; Grasso et al., 2011) and educating about the general effects of trauma and the specific effects of different kinds of trauma, such as sexual abuse (Cohen et al., 2004). A study of parents and their children who had mood disorders found that psychoeducation helped the parents seek better services for their child, and that as these services were identified, the children had a corresponding decrease in symptom severity (Mendenhall, Fristad, & Early, 2009). Psychoeducation to children in the aftermath of a traumatic event has also been shown to be effective in reducing symptom severity (Scheeringa et al., 2010; Silverman et al., 2008).

### Therapeutic Alliance

One of the most important tasks early in therapy with traumatized youths is building rapport and a strong therapeutic alliance (Cloitre, Chase Stovall-McClough, Miranda, & Chemtob, 2004; Cohen et al., 2012). Support from the therapist can help the child manage the difficult therapeutic tasks that lie ahead (Chemtob et al., 2002b). The strength of the therapeutic alliance between the therapist and the patient has been found to be a predictor of PTSD symptom improvement in adult survivors of childhood abuse (Cloitre et al., 2004). Building a strong alliance is particularly important with youths who have undergone several traumas because they are more likely to view relationships as unstable or threatening (Cohen et al., 2012).

### Termination Process

Termination of therapy can be a difficult time for all children, but may be particularly difficult for traumatized kids who have prior experience with loss (Many, 2009; Silva et al., 2000). It is therefore important to begin the termination discussion early during treatment and to recruit parents to facilitate the termination process (Many, 2009; Silva et al., 2003). The final sessions of exposure therapy should focus on summarizing, reviewing, reinforcing, and promoting generalization of the exposure and the coping and emotional control skills gained through therapy (Cohen et al., 2012).

Other goals of the termination process include evaluating the progress made in treatment (Deblinger, McLeer, & Henry, 1990) and emphasizing the child's achievements (Silva et al., 2000). The therapist should communicate clearly that there is a potential for symptoms to recur and that "booster sessions" may be needed to prevent relapse (Many, 2009). The therapist must also address any other preexisting disorders and their treatment, and provide the child and caregiver with referrals if necessary (Silva et al., 2000).

### Other Techniques

In addition to these components, several other techniques have been applied successfully in treating young trauma survivors. Some studies have used a more expressive therapeutic approach and have shown success in treating posttraumatic symptoms (Chemtob et al., 2002b), whereas others have included parental training and/or treatment in addition to child CBT, resulting in positive effects in both the children and the parents (Silverman et al., 2008). These parental training components involve education, child behavior management skills, and coping skills for their emotional struggles (Overbeek, de Schipper, Lamers-Winkelman, & Schuengel, 2012; Silverman et al., 2008).

Trauma intervention can also include educating survivors about the complex interaction of cognition, affect, and physiology in the etiology of PTSD symptoms (King et al., 2000). The relationship of thoughts, feelings, and behaviors can also be explored (Cohen et al., 2004) through asking patients to describe what they thought, felt, and did during stressful situations (Farrell, Hains, & Davies, 1998), and by exploring the relationship of negative cognitions to negative emotions and behaviors (Cohen et al., 2000). Child interventions have included education in identifying trauma-related emotions and understanding their links to thoughts, physiological responses, and behavior (Deblinger et al., 2001; Farrell et al., 1998). Several therapies also include training in managing and expressing trauma-related feelings adaptively such as anxiety, anger, and grief (Chemtob et al., 2002a; Deblinger et al., 1990; March et al., 1998). Emotional regulation and social skills training are important aspects of trauma intervention that have been shown to facilitate approach rather than avoidance (Cloitre et al., 2004; Cloitre, Koenen, Cohen, & Han, 2002; Dorsey et al., 2011).

## Risks and Benefits of This Treatment Program

CCT incorporates several unique components that render it distinguishable from other interventions for trauma-exposed youth. First, the use of a life timeline helps address the impact of accumulated experiences, examining the direct influence of circumscribed traumatic events as well as other daily or life stressors. Second, youths and caregivers learn the conditioning process that led to the symptoms and are invited to evaluate it when experiencing both cues and their responses to cues. As the child identifies cues associated with this conditioning and develops more adaptive responses to them, she acquires self-efficacy and feels empowered. Third, through the use of insight-oriented strategies and visual icons linking history, emotions, and behaviors, the child is challenged to avoid compartmentalization of these constructs, and problem behaviors are placed in an empathic context. In addition to using behavioral, cognitive, and emotional approaches to develop new responses, CCT incorporates a physiological approach (i.e., how the child feels physically), recognizing that many children who experience trauma are sensitive to their interoceptive cues (e.g., increased heart rate, sweating).

### Variability of Trauma Outcomes

If left untreated, childhood problems resulting from trauma may become chronic and persist into adolescence and adulthood, such as increased suicide attempts, substance abuse, and depression (Abram et al., 2004; Cohen, Mannarino, Perel, & Staron, 2007). A large amount of variability has been found throughout the course of childhood PTSD, with some children showing a delayed reaction, others showing an early reaction and a gradual decrease over time, others showing consistently high symptomology, and still others demonstrating a high relapse rate after initial recovery (Terranova et al., 2009). Treatment algorithms need to be developed for children who experience trauma. We need to continue to develop treatments that can become more focused and targeted to specific populations that differ in presentation, course, and outcome.

### Working with Traumatized Youths

This CCT manual was written for mental health professionals (i.e., psychologists, psychiatrists, social workers, and school therapists) who have experience working with traumatized youths and a familiarity with evidence-based interventions for childhood trauma. Given the specific skill set required for trauma intervention, we do not recommend that individuals without mental health training use this manual. It is highly advisable that professionals who wish to become proficient in CCT receive training on the manual before using the intervention. Our group is currently developing a training program.

Working with traumatized youths can be very rewarding; however, it also presents many challenges. Exposure to others' trauma stories over time can affect even the most seasoned of professionals. Thus, for those of us who treat traumatized populations, it is important to monitor our own levels of stress to prevent vicarious traumatization. Symptoms of vicarious traumatization may resemble those of direct trauma, including intrusive imagery or thoughts, physiological arousal, avoidance, or anxiety. It may also disrupt personal or professional relationships. The American Psychological Association and International Society for Traumatic Stress Studies offer advice on prevention of vicarious traumatization. Suggestions include engaging in proper self-care, such as eating healthy foods, getting enough rest and exercise, engaging in relaxing activities (e.g., listening to music, meditating, being out in nature), recognizing your limits, enlisting consultation or supervision as needed, and watching for signs of burnout (e.g., exhaustion, numbing, distancing, overinvolvement with clients). Our team engages in frequent group discussions, mindfulness exercises, and encouragement of personal time. During our discussions we share challenging scenarios, but we balance these with successful stories and clinical vignettes that illustrate progress in therapy.

## Alternative Treatments

A number of treatment protocols have been developed for treating posttraumatic symptoms in children. TF-CBT has numerous randomized controlled trials supporting its validity and efficacy in the treatment of trauma in youths (Cohen & Mannarino, 2008; Cohen, Mannarino, & Knudsen, 2005; Scheeringa et al., 2011). Initially developed for the treatment of sexual trauma, TF-CBT has demonstrated to be effective in reducing PTSD symptoms among youths exposed to intimate partner violence (Cohen, Mannarino, & Iyengar, 2011a). Multimodality trauma treatment, a group cognitive–behavioral intervention, has been shown to be effective in community mental health and school settings (Amaya-Jackson et al., 2003). Child–parent psychotherapy combines play with other modalities to restore attachment and regulate traumatic stress in young children (Ghosh Ippen, Harris, Van Horn, & Lieberman, 2011). Other treatments that have shown promise for reducing posttraumatic stress symptoms in trauma-exposed youths include eye movement desensitization and reprocessing, and systems therapy (Chaffin & Friedrich, 2004; Chemtob, Nakashima, & Hamada, 2002b; Ellis et al., 2012).

Cognitive behavioral intervention for trauma in schools (CBITS) was developed out of the concern that, although other treatment protocols have adequate treatment effects, their practice in the real world can be challenging (Langley, Nadeem, Kataoka, Stein, & Jaycox, 2010). In school settings, CBITS adds elements targeting ease of implementation and adherence to groups of children.

### Individual Versus Group Modalities

Although there is still little consensus regarding whether individual or group modalities are best suited to working with traumatized populations, some evidence does suggest that individual treatments are superior. A study comparing individual and group therapy for sexually abused girls found that, although the two conditions did not differ in general functioning after therapy, the individual condition showed more improvement in posttraumatic symptoms (Trowell et al., 2002). A meta-analysis of psychosocial treatments for youths exposed to violence found that group CBT in a school setting reduced symptoms of PTSD compared with a waitlist group (Silverman et al., 2008). Other group therapies were not found to be more effective at reducing symptoms than waitlist controls.

CCT and CBITS share an emphasis on recurring traumas and the acknowledgment that parents may not be available for treatment for all sessions; however, unlike CBITS, CCT is an individual treatment rather than a group intervention. Although group interventions are cost-effective, it is necessary to emphasize individual history, feelings, behaviors, and cues.

The field of developmental traumatology is moving in the direction of individualized treatment. The goal of the field is to develop treatment algorithms that focus on different populations and are not limited to a narrow set of approaches for a heterogeneous group. CCT aims to target those children and adolescents with a chronic history of trauma, adversity, and ongoing stress.

### Complexity and Insight

The availability of interventions such as TF-CBT and CBITS has had a significant impact on the successful treatment of traumatized children. Treatment availability, however, remains limited for such a complex problem as pediatric PTSD. The development of new treatments is necessary to address the complex manifestations of posttraumatic symptoms, particularly for children with histories of ongoing stress, adversity, and trauma who need interventions tailored especially to their experience. Processing an isolated event may not address the core conflict experienced by chronically traumatized children, such as youths in inner cities exposed to ongoing violence. Children need to be empowered through knowledge (insight) into how the consequences of their experiences may be reflected in their symptoms and behaviors. CCT was developed in recognition of the growing need for a manualized treatment that aims to increase youths' insight into how a history of trauma may relate to current emotions, and how these in turn may be linked to maladaptive behaviors.

## Outline of This Treatment Program

CCT consists of 15 sessions divided into four phases, as listed in the table of contents and as detailed here. Phase 1 (sessions 1–3) prepares the child or adolescent and caregivers for exposure through education and coping skills training. The psychoeducation and mindfulness, relaxation, and cognitive skill training received during phase 1 help prepare children for the exposure to the life story examination and the evaluation of cues that occur during subsequent phases. They also provide children with tools to use when confronted with traumatic reminders, intrusive thoughts, and anxiety outside of therapy.

During phase 2 (sessions 4–7), the youth tells her life story, highlighting both positive and negative events as a form of narrative exposure. During sessions 4 and 5, the therapist listens empathically, helping to identify cognitions, emotions, cues, and memory gaps. During sessions 6 and 7, the therapist and the child work together to restructure cognitive distortions and misattributions. The cues identified during phase 2 become the focus for the next phase of treatment.

During phase 3 (sessions 8–12), the therapist, the youth, and caregivers work together to identify cues and reduce the associated negative responses. Exposure to the cues occurs in three stages: imaginary, in session, and in vivo. After exposure, the therapist works with the youth to identify solutions to obstacles encountered when using new coping tools. Last, during phase 4 (sessions 13–15), the youth is encouraged to use all her learned skills to develop a coherent life narrative, and the therapist, child, and caregiver work to ensure that treatment gains are sustained after therapy.

Within the confines delineated in this manual, individual therapists have the flexibility to tailor the treatment as necessary for each youth. Individual factors such as age, developmental level, cultural background, current functioning, progress in therapy, and numerous other factors can influence delivery and should be considered. For example, when working with young children, art therapy may be used as a tool to facilitate the objectives of a session.

Sessions generally occur once a week for 45 minutes; however, the therapist may adapt the time to meet the individual needs of the child. One to two additional sessions may be added to each phase if the youth is having difficulty grasping the concepts of that phase. Sessions are intended to build on one another, thus the therapist should not advance to a later session without ensuring the child has mastered prior material.

## Phase 1

### Session 1: Education (Youth and Caregivers)

Caretakers and the youth acquire knowledge on the psychological aftermath of trauma, the long-term consequences of not addressing the trauma, and the benefits of treatment. The therapist provides a conceptualization of trauma and the treatment process, and describes the structure of the CCT treatment.

### Sessions 2 and 3: Mindfulness, Relaxation, and Cognitive Tools

The youth is provided resources that she may use when exploring the life timeline by learning how to be more mindful, practicing relaxation exercises, and applying cognitive coping skills. The therapist teaches skills, emphasizes the importance of daily practice, and helps the youth develop her own coping tools.

## Phase 2

### Sessions 4 and 5: Chronic Traumatic Stress History

The therapist acts as an active and empathetic listener, encouraging the youth to begin to verbalize her experiences, identifying cognitive distortions within her narrative and details of the traumatic events (sensations, visuals, context) that may be acting as cues. The three key emotions of anger, sadness, and fear are examined within the narrative and are redefined to the youth as necessary.

### Sessions 6 and 7: Processing of the Chronic Traumatic Stress History

The child is encouraged to redefine her role as a survivor rather than a victim, beginning the process of cognitive restructuring. The therapist assists in verbalizing key emotions while providing hope, correcting cognitive distortions, and attempting to fill in memory gaps. In addition, the therapist helps the child fit chronic traumatic events into the larger narrative of her life, identifying areas where the child has control for reconstruction of her story.

## Phase 3

### Session 8: Midtherapy Update (Youth and Caregivers)

Ideally, the child experiences caregiver engagement during the therapeutic process. Caregivers are informed about the methods and progress of therapy, with the goal of understanding their key role in the treatment process. The therapist provides the child with positive feedback on her work in therapy, facilitates the child's role as the main informant on her progress, and prepares caretakers to act as facilitators during the next phase of treatment. Progress at this point is evaluated clinically.

### Session 9: Approaching Cues

The child's new ways of thinking and feeling about the trauma are reinforced, and a consensus is obtained about which cues she wants to address. The therapist helps the child understand what happens at four different levels—emotionally, physically, cognitively, and behaviorally—when she is exposed to cues.

### Session 10: Imaginary Exposure to Cues

The child begins to identify emotional, cognitive, and physical responses that result from reexperiencing cues. The therapist teaches applications of new coping tools and gauges the child's level of emotional distress continually.

### Session 11: Within-Session Exposure to Cues

The youth manages the emotional, cognitive, and physical challenges that result from cue exposure. The therapist actively exposes the child to identified cues through role-playing and simulation, demonstrating empathy, showing the youth understanding, and reinforcing further the idea that the youth is not to blame for trauma-related symptoms.

### Session 12: Evaluation of in Vivo Exposure Assignment

The youth is assisted in developing a new repertoire of responses to trauma cues. The therapist identifies new tools as well as obstacles while beginning to discuss termination, or "graduation," issues.

## Phase 4

### Session 13: Processing the Chronic Traumatic Stress History

The child expresses verbally how she survived the negative events of her life, as well as indicates her thoughts and emotions about all adverse events. The therapist evaluates the youth's progress in therapy and provides empathy and positive reinforcement on the work that has been done so far.

### Session 14: Closing Session 1 (Youth and Caregivers)

Caretakers are provided final clinical observations, results of treatment, and future recommendations. The therapist discusses clinical progress and the potential need for treatment of comorbid conditions or future posttraumatic symptom reoccurrences.

### Session 15: Closing Session 2 (Youth Only)

The therapist provides the child with positive feedback, helps the child know what to do when confronted with future challenges, and reviews therapeutic gains. The child is educated on how to retain those gains and get help if needed in the future.

# CHAPTER 2 Diagnostic Criteria and Assessment

## Assessment Recommendations

Assessment of child trauma survivors must be developmentally sensitive and include multiple reporters in a clinical interview (Cohen et al., 2012; Donnelly & Amaya-Jackson, 2002). Finkelhor and colleagues suggest a need to question youths about a broad spectrum of victimization experiences (Finkelhor, Ormrod, Turner, & Hamby, 2005), whereas the American Academy of Child and Adolescent Psychiatry (AACAP) highlights the importance of assessing the degree of child impairment resulting from PTSD symptoms (Schneider et al., 2013). Assessment should include general questions about the child's psychological health and functioning as well as specific inquires about the trauma history and symptoms (Cohen, Berliner, & Mannarino, 2010). The use of standardized assessment instruments can provide a baseline by which to measure treatment gains and are a means to identify other lifetime traumatic events (Finkelhor et al., 2005; Schneider et al., 2013).

### Recognizing PTSD Symptoms

The DSM-V update on PTSD diagnosis accounts for developmental variations in symptom manifestation (American Psychiatric Association, 2013), including a separate subtype for children younger than 6 years of age.

#### PTSD in Preschool Children

Three symptoms are required to diagnose PTSD in preschool children (Box 2.1). Intrusive recollections do not need to be distressing, as in the

### Box 2.1 Diagnostic Criteria for Pediatric PTSD

Below we list the *DSM-5* criteria for PTSD in children, adolescents and adults. Please note that the *DSM-5* introduced a separate description for children ages six years and younger.

#### Criterion A: stressor

The person was exposed to: death, threatened death, actual or threatened serious injury, or actual or threatened sexual violence, as follows: **(one required)**

1. Direct exposure.
2. Witnessing, in person.
3. Indirectly, by learning that a close relative or close friend was exposed to trauma. If the event involved actual or threatened death, it must have been violent or accidental.
4. Repeated or extreme indirect exposure to aversive details of the event(s), usually in the course of professional duties (e.g., first responders, collecting body parts; professionals repeatedly exposed to details of child abuse). This does not include indirect non-professional exposure through electronic media, television, movies, or pictures.

#### Criterion B: intrusion symptoms

The traumatic event is persistently re-experienced in the following way(s): **(one required)**

1. Recurrent, involuntary, and intrusive memories. Note: Children older than six may express this symptom in repetitive play.
2. Traumatic nightmares. Note: Children may have frightening dreams without content related to the trauma(s).
3. Dissociative reactions (e.g., flashbacks) which may occur on a continuum from brief episodes to complete loss of consciousness. Note: Children may reenact the event in play.
4. Intense or prolonged distress after exposure to traumatic reminders.
5. Marked physiologic reactivity after exposure to trauma-related stimuli.

#### Criterion C: avoidance

Persistent effortful avoidance of distressing trauma-related stimuli after the event: **(one required)**

1. Trauma-related thoughts or feelings.

2. Trauma-related external reminders (e.g., people, places, conversations, activities, objects, or situations).

### Criterion D: negative alterations in cognitions and mood

Negative alterations in cognitions and mood that began or worsened after the traumatic event: **(two required)**

1. Inability to recall key features of the traumatic event (usually dissociative amnesia; not due to head injury, alcohol, or drugs).
2. Persistent (and often distorted) negative beliefs and expectations about oneself or the world (e.g., "I am bad," "The world is completely dangerous").
3. Persistent distorted blame of self or others for causing the traumatic event or for resulting consequences.
4. Persistent negative trauma-related emotions (e.g., fear, horror, anger, guilt, or shame).
5. Markedly diminished interest in (pre-traumatic) significant activities.
6. Feeling alienated from others (e.g., detachment or estrangement).
7. Constricted affect: persistent inability to experience positive emotions.

### Criterion E: alterations in arousal and reactivity

Trauma-related alterations in arousal and reactivity that began or worsened after the traumatic event: **(two required)**

1. Irritable or aggressive behavior
2. Self-destructive or reckless behavior
3. Hypervigilence
4. Exaggerated startle response
5. Problems in concentration
6. Sleep disturbance

### Criterion F: duration

Persistence of symptoms (in Criteria B, C, D, and E) for more than one month.

### Criterion G: functional significance

Significant symptom-related distress or functional impairment (e.g., social, occupational).

### Criterion H: exclusion

Disturbance is not due to medication, substance use, or other illness.

*Specify if*: With dissociative symptoms.

In addition to meeting criteria for diagnosis, an individual experiences high levels of either of the following in reaction to trauma-related stimuli:

1. **Depersonalization**: experience of being an outside observer of or detached from oneself (e.g., feeling as if "this is not happening to me" or one were in a dream).
2. **Derealization**: experience of unreality, distance, or distortion (e.g., "things are not real").

*Specify if*: With delayed expression.

Full diagnosis is not met until at least six months after the trauma(s), although onset of symptoms may occur immediately.



adult criteria. Because young children cannot necessarily verbalize their feelings, detachment and estrangement criteria have been reworded to "socially withdrawn." Preschool-age children need only one symptom of avoidance or numbing instead of the three that were required in DSM-IV because they are limited in their ability to express internalized symptoms such as a sense of a foreshortened future. In addition, the DSM-IV criterion for irritability and anger outbursts has been altered for preschoolers to include extreme temper tantrums, and the requirement for diminished interest in significant activities has been broadened to include restrictions in play and social interactions.

## PTSD in Youths

Symptoms of PTSD manifest differently in young people. Children may engage in repetitive play and may experience frightening dreams without specific content (Dyregrov & Yule, 2006). Many children develop fears associated with certain aspects of traumas that may develop into phobias

(Perrin, Smith, & Yule, 2000). Children with PTSD often experience guilt over what they should or could have done in a particular situation (Kletter et al., 2009). A number of cognitive problems have also been observed in traumatized youths. Children with PTSD frequently report difficulties in concentration, especially with regard to schoolwork (Rust & Troupe, 1991), possibly developing memory problems in both learning new material and in remembering previously acquired skills.

### PTSD in Older Children and Adults

PTSD criteria for older children and adults have been modified in the DSM-V to include a broader understanding of exposure (e.g., learning about threats from others, recurrent exposure to aversive details). In addition, dissociative reactions and frightening dreams without recognizable content are included on the symptoms under cluster B. Avoidance and numbing are divided into their own clusters. The following symptoms have been added to the DSM-V: persistent and exaggerated negative expectations about one's self, others, or the world; persistent distorted blame of self or others about the cause or consequences of the traumatic event(s); pervasive negative emotional state (e.g., fear, horror, anger, guilt, shame); and reckless or self-destructive behavior (American Psychiatric Association, 2013).

## Understanding How Trauma Leads to PTSD

The harmful effects of trauma are believed to develop through a combination of behavioral, cognitive, and physiological processes. A behavioral theory posits that traumatic symptoms result from hyperactivation of the normal fear response (Elsesser, Sartory, & Tackenberg, 2004). According to this theory, the initial exposure to a traumatic event activates a startle response that consists of physiological arousal and a behavioral response (such as fight or flight). Through the process of fear conditioning, the elements of the trauma that cause the sensation of fear directly (the unconditioned stimuli) become paired with neutral elements present in the environment at the time of the trauma (the conditioned stimuli), leading to a sense of fear when presented with formerly neutral stimuli (conditioned response) (Fani et al., 2012; Mowrer, 1960). Thus, neutral stimuli come to serve as cues that trigger traumatic memories, reexperience, arousal, and avoidance. Trauma causes a normal fear reaction to be overactivated to such a degree that normal habituation and extinction fail to occur (Fani et al., 2012). This fear response to traumatic stimuli may increase over time and, through cross-sensitization, may even generalize to new stimuli (Inslicht et al., 2013).

### Behavioral Responses

A survivor may attempt to avoid any stimuli associated with the trauma, causing memories to remain unprocessed and to resurface in the form of flashbacks and intrusive thoughts (Brewin & Holmes, 2003; Ehlers & Clark, 2000). The association between trauma cues and fear or threat is strong, with cues continuing to elicit posttraumatic symptoms long after the trauma (Dalgleish, 2004; Dunmore, Clark, & Ehlers, 2001). Cues have the power to cause physiological arousal, activate negative cognitive appraisals and schemas, invoke feelings such as fear and anxiety, and cause avoidance and hyperarousal behaviors (Dalgleish, 2004; Dunmore et al., 2001). These responses can be conceptualized as the individual attempts to manage the threat caused by the stimulus. For example, when a child in a classroom responds to loud noise by running away, he is attempting to manage what his body perceives as a threat. That behavioral response was likely adapted to a once real, threatening situation; however, it is now maladaptive and leads to further problems. In this case, the loud noise is the conditioned stimulus; the reaction of running away is the conditioned response.

### Traumatic Memories

Traumatic memories are stored in an associative network, or fear structure, containing information about the traumatic event and its sequelae, response patterns, and the individual's interpretation of the traumatic stimuli (Dalgleish, 2004; Dunmore et al., 2001). The memories contained in a trauma network are often qualitatively different than ordinary memories. They are often experienced in the present and tend to be more sensory, more resistant to subsequent learning, and more vulnerable to stimuli that are temporally, rather than semantically, linked to the original event (Bedard-Gilligan & Zoellner, 2012; Brewin & Holmes, 2003; Ehlers & Clark, 2000). Trauma memories are also less likely to be well elaborated and integrated into autobiographical memory, context, and other knowledge because they are fragmented (Bedard-Gilligan & Zoellner, 2012; Ehlers & Clark, 2000), meaning the child may recall the sense of threat without clearly discerning its origin.

Pathological trauma reactions occur when excessive stress or avoidance results in a failure of the transfer of memories from sensory to verbal memory, leaving traumatic memories that are unprocessed, unintegrated, and triggered involuntarily by situational cues and sensory stimuli (Bedard-Gilligan & Zoellner, 2012; Brewin & Holmes, 2003). If the child stores a sensation rather than a verbal narrative, he will retrieve the sensation and not the verbal memory. Children that dissociate during trauma, a normal adaptive response at times, may be at increased risk of having these memory disturbances because they do not completely capture the meaning of the event (Bedard-Gilligan & Zoellner, 2012). The resulting sensory processing may contribute to the verbal memory deficits experienced by many children exposed to trauma. In general, children who have experienced interpersonal trauma have lower verbal and full-scale IQ scores (Carrey, Butter, Persinger, & Bialik, 1995; Saltzman, Weems, & Carrion, 2006). Furthermore, the dose and severity of the trauma and the degree of posttraumatic symptoms and impairment have strong negative correlations to verbal and full-scale IQ scores (Brewin & Holmes, 2003; Saltzman et al., 2006). Visual IQ seems not to be affected in the same way, underscoring the importance of icons and visual materials during the early phases of treatment.

### Physiological Processes

Physiological processes accompany the fear conditioning process. A normal stress response results in the activation of the sympathetic nervous system and its central adrenergic mechanisms (de Kloet et al., 2006). Upon removal of a stressful situation, these physiological processes return to homeostasis, the tendency we all have to maintain stability in our systems. In the case of ongoing trauma, however, these systems remain activated as the threat continues. This pathological stress response is associated with the dysregulation of the limbic–hypothalamic–pituitary–adrenal axis (Carrion et al., 2002a). The activation of this neuroendocrine chain results in cortisol release and has been linked to the stress response (autonomic activation, behavioral arousal) and to learning and memory (conditioning, habituation, and extinction) (Brewin & Saunders, 2001; de Kloet et al., 2006).

### Cognitive Appraisals and Distortions

These behavioral and physiological processes are also accompanied by cognitive appraisals of the traumatic event, its cause, its repercussions, and the survivor's perception of his own and others' role in the event (Ehlers & Clark, 2000). These appraisals about the traumatic event and its aftermath help determine what emotions a child experiences, what he remembers about it, and what behavioral and cognitive strategies he uses when exposed to cues (Dunmore et al., 2001; Ehlers & Clark, 2000). Negative cognitive attributions and attributional styles after trauma are correlated with the development of depression, anxiety, dissociation, social problems, negative emotions such as anger and guilt, and posttraumatic symptoms (Brewin & Holmes, 2003; Cohen & Mannarino, 2000; Ehlers, Mayou, & Bryant, 2003).

Cognitive distortions arise when a trauma survivor attempts to make sense of the traumatic experience and his role (Cohen, Mannarino, Berliner, & Deblinger, 2000), and from trying to fit it into preexisting cognitive schemas (Brewin & Holmes, 2003; Dalgleish, 2004). The new information received from the trauma must somehow fit into their prior worldview or, alternately, the worldview must be altered to match the trauma information (Brewin & Holmes, 2003). According to the theory of shattered assumptions, updating a worldview to fit this new information can lead to reexperiencing the trauma and also avoidance of the memories (Brewin & Holmes, 2003). As a result of their cognitive developmental level, children may be particularly likely to develop distorted thoughts after traumatic experiences (Cohen et al., 2000). These distortions may include survivor's guilt, self-blame, a sense of responsibility for the trauma, omen formation, a view of oneself as different from others, a lack of trust, and the development of a view that the world is a dangerous place (Brewin & Holmes, 2003; Cohen et al., 2000).

### Emotional Dysregulation

According to cognitive theory, emotions and thoughts are linked intimately. Distorted cognitions can lead to negative emotional states and behaviors, such as depression, anxiety, and PTSD (Beck, 1976). After a traumatic event, thoughts and memories related to the trauma may be accompanied by strong secondary emotions, such as guilt and anger (Brewin & Holmes, 2003; Dalgleish, 2004; Dunmore et al., 2001), which results in trauma memories being continually processed emotionally, rather than logically and verbally. These negative emotional states result in symptom maintenance (Brewin & Holmes, 2003).

Emotions are stored within an integrated network of memory, thought, and behavioral responses (Pollak, Cicchetti, & Klorman, 1998). Traumatized children come to associate any stimuli that evoke certain emotions with the traumatic experience, and thus with a sense of threat and their accompanying behavioral responses (Dalgleish, 2004). Emotional dysregulation may include emotional lability, increased negative emotionality, socially inappropriate emotional expression, and a lack of strategies for coping with emotion (Dalgleish, 2004; Shipman & Zeman, 2001). Given their lack of coping skills, children learn to avoid situations or cues that lead to strong emotions (Dalgleish, 2004).

### Other Factors

In addition to these cognitive–behavioral influences, several other factors are correlated to children's posttraumatic symptom severity. Proximity to the traumatic event, frequency of violence, prior history of trauma exposure, and prior psychopathology influence both the development of PTSD symptoms and their intensity (Dalgleish, 2004; Daviss et al., 2000; Ruf et al., 2010; Silva et al., 2000).

Caregivers' emotional distress and lack of child-perceived support after trauma influence depression, anxiety, posttraumatic symptoms, and externalizing behaviors in traumatized children (Dalgleish, 2004; Daviss et al., 2000). If children sense their caregivers do not believe their account of the trauma, this may also influence the severity of their distress. Measures of overall family functioning such as conflict and adaptability have also been correlated with internalizing problems in child trauma survivors (Cohen & Mannarino, 2000). Girls may be more likely to report internalizing symptoms, including depression and anxiety, whereas boys may report more externalizing symptoms, such as aggression and conduct issues (Buckner, Beardslee, & Bassuk, 2004). The reactions that caregivers have when they learn about their child's trauma and the caregivers' support of the child influence the outcome of treatment (Cohen et al., 2011; Schneider et al., 2013).

# CHAPTER 3 Assessment of the Child

*This session should be conducted with the youth and the caregiver.*

## MATERIALS NEEDED

- Traumatic Experiences Supplemental Form
- Cue-Centered Therapy Assessment Note-Taking Form (optional)
- Consent and assent forms for this meeting (recommended) if administering the protocol as part of a clinical trial

## OUTLINE

- Conduct a clinical interview with the child and the caregiver. If the child is at a developmental age of 15 years or older, it is recommended the child be interviewed first, then the caregiver. Supplement this interview with specific trauma-related questions.
- Assess the caregiver for impact of chronic traumatic stress and evaluate family support system.

***Note***: Standardized measures may be used to supplement the information obtained during this session. Descriptions of common childhood trauma assessment measures can be found in the National Child Traumatic Stress Network (NCTSN) Measures Review Database (www.nctsn.org/resources/online-research/measures-review).

## Session Overview

### Goals

- Get a thorough history of the child's life (from birth to this visit). Ask about events that caused traumatic stress and
  - how these events affected the child
  - how she is currently functioning
  - what posttraumatic symptoms she is experiencing
  - how the caregivers are affected by chronic traumatic stress
- Evaluate the child's familial and community support systems.

### Therapist's Role

- Building a rapport
- Listening empathically
- Beginning of case formulation and treatment plan

## Clinical Interview

The assessment should include both caregiver and child, and they should be interviewed separately as well as jointly. Usually, adolescents are more comfortable discussing certain issues without the caregiver present, such as substance abuse, sexuality, eating disorders, and peer issues. After a joint introduction to the session, the adolescent should be seen first. This strategy provides the adolescent with feelings of ownership and independence, which are crucial at this age. If the caregiver seems to require special clinical attention or specifically requests a separate interview, set aside time for her to voice her concerns. Confidentiality issues should be addressed, assuring the child confidentiality for issues that do not place her at further risk.

The initial assessment consists of a series of questions regarding development and chronic history of trauma and stress in addition to standard questions for a clinical intake evaluation interview. The assessment should cover the youth's functioning across multiple domains, including social, academic, developmental, medical history, and family history, as well as an evaluation of the youth's current mental status. During this initial interview, start delineating the significant life events in the youth's life and pay particular attention to adversities and traumatic events. In addition, assess the child's and family's adaptive styles to these stressors. Noting life events and functioning, including additional diagnoses that may not appear to be related to trauma, is also relevant in terms of subsequent impact. For clinical use, you may photocopy the Traumatic Experiences Supplemental Form (Worksheet 3.1) and the Cue-Centered Therapy Assessment Note-Taking Form (Worksheet 3.2) at the end of this session. Here is a case example:

*Johnny has been diagnosed with ADHD. He often gets in trouble at home for not listening to his mother when she asks him to turn off the TV. Johnny's mother often feels overwhelmed. She screams a lot and tells him that things are "all his fault" because he is so difficult. There is a history of aggression in the family. Johnny's condition, in combination with the family's level of functioning, makes him more likely to experience physical abuse. If he does experience such abuse, his treatment will also be complicated by his preexisting ADHD.*

Although eliciting trauma-related material is a crucial step in individualizing treatment, many therapists do not ask trauma-related questions, or, if they do, they do not ask for enough detail. A sufficiently detailed understanding provides the basis on which the therapy is built. The better your understanding of the child and his history, the better equipped you will be in supporting the child's work in identifying cues, developing coping tools, and developing new responses to those cues.

### Who, What, Where, When, Why, and How

When talking about the youth's traumatic events, it is important to learn about the Five Ws (and one H) of journalism: Who, What, Where, When, Why, and How. Think of yourself as a journalist inasmuch as you are trying to get an objective record of the symptoms the child is currently experiencing without making premature judgments about their origins. Note the symptoms, but keep an open mind and do not assume they are all trauma related. As you continue to work with the child, the appropriate links between symptoms and trauma history will become evident.

If the child appears reluctant to discuss the traumatic events, do not attempt to force the process at this point in therapy. Rather, focus on themes that relate to experiences the youth is willing to discuss. It is important to identify the details of the traumatic events brought up during the interview. For example, if the caregiver explains the child experiences community violence, find out in detail what this means—what is she actually seeing and hearing, how frequently is she exposed, and how close is she to the perpetrators and victims. Here is a case example:

*Sam lives next door to a couple who argues frequently. Sam is often awoken at night by screams heard through the walls. It is important to assess how well Sam knows this couple and whether he is exposed to the aftermath of their fights (e.g., he sees the woman with a black eye the next day). It is important to gain an understanding of how the rest of the family responds to hearing the screaming. One must also assess whether there is any history of violence within Sam's own family.*

During the assessment, it is crucial to listen actively and elicit trauma-related material without making any therapeutic interventions, although there may be a strong desire to do so. The goal at this stage is not to begin correcting cognitive distortions or to provide empathy, but rather to gain an understanding of the traumatic history and its effects. Listening without intervention allows the child and the caregiver to feel heard and understood. Intervention at this point might instead lead the youth to believe that her stories are "wrong" or "incorrect," and she may become reluctant to express her own perspective. The child may also want to protect the therapist from other serious accounts that may be difficult to disclose early during treatment.

### Assessment across Multiple Domains

The assessment should not only consist of obtaining accounts of chronic traumatic stress, but also it should explore how these events have affected the child across multiple domains:

- **Development**: Was there ever a change in the child's play or socialization? Was there ever an impact on achievement or maintenance of developmental milestones?
- **Biology**: Have sleep, appetite, and growth been affected?
- **Resiliency**: What are the child's strengths that have helped her cope with chronic traumatic stress?

- **Support systems**: Have interactions with family, friends, and peers changed at any point in time?

The assessment should also provide an appraisal of the youth's openness and readiness for therapy, as well as her ability to complete required tasks. Estimates of the youth's motivation, intelligence, and insight, based on overall interactions and impressions, can help determine whether the therapy is a suitable match. This information may allow you to foresee potential difficulties during the course of treatment.

## Assessment of Caregiver and Family System

Family support is a key factor in determining a child's severity of symptoms and progress in therapy. As part of the clinical interview, assess the impact of chronic traumatic stress on the caregiver and family system. Meet with the caregiver separately from the child as needed. A history from caregivers about themselves may help elucidate important facts that are now part of the child's chronic traumatic stress history. Assess risk factors in the caregiver for posttraumatic reactions, such as previous history of anxiety, early life trauma, and adversities. Also assess their strengths and resilient factors; these will be helpful when asking the caregiver to assist the child with the sessions. Here is a case example:

*Maggie brings her son Billy for therapy because of nightmares he has experienced ever since their house was flooded. Although Billy appears to be suffering the most, the entire family was affected by the flood, losing belongings and having their lives destabilized. Maggie herself has been under stress from struggling to cope with loss and rebuilding the family's life. It is important to attend to and address Maggie's concerns as well as Billy's to help her be the supportive parent he needs.*

### Caregivers' Recognition of Trauma

The assessment of traumatic events and the assessment of the child's function prepare the family to recognize that these events will be the focus of treatment. Caregivers may underestimate the impact of traumatic events on their child. The caregivers may be traumatized knowing what their child has experienced and may use avoidance as a psychological defense to protect themselves from the pain of acknowledging the trauma.

Caregivers often struggle with a desire to deny or minimize what happened to their child, and with their own feelings of guilt over their failure to keep their child safe or not to provide a better environment for their child. Because of the potential for caregivers to underestimate the impact of trauma, it is crucial the therapist convey in a supportive manner the far-reaching effects of chronic traumatic stress.

**Worksheet 3.1**

## Traumatic Experiences Supplemental Form

*Instructions*: Please complete each field when working with the child.

☐ **Identify Traumatic Experiences**

For each identified event ask:

What happened?

________________________________________

________________________________________

Who did it?

________________________________________

________________________________________

When did it happen?

________________________________________

________________________________________

Where did it happen?

________________________________________

________________________________________

How did the child feel before it happened? While it was happening? Afterward?

________________________________________

________________________________________

________________________________________

What was the level of family functioning before it happened? While it was happening? Afterward?

______________________________________________

______________________________________________

______________________________________________

## ☐ Identify What Is Happening Now in the Youth's Life

Socially? (Any new anxieties?)

______________________________________________

______________________________________________

______________________________________________

Academically? (Has performance declined?)

______________________________________________

______________________________________________

______________________________________________

Developmentally? (Any signs of regression?)

______________________________________________

______________________________________________

______________________________________________

## ☐ Evaluate Mental Status

Mood/affect ______________________________________

Thought process/content ____________________________

Insight/judgment ___________________________________________

Suicidality/homicidality ______________________________________

Presence of any hallucinations, delusions, obsessions, compulsions________________

______________________________________________________

☐ **Acquire Social, School, and Medical History**

Evaluate current support in the following areas:

Family: _______________________________________________

______________________________________________________

______________________________________________________

______________________________________________________

Friends: _______________________________________________

______________________________________________________

______________________________________________________

______________________________________________________

School system: __________________________________________

______________________________________________________

______________________________________________________

______________________________________________________

Community: ____________________________________________

______________________________________________________

Health system: ______

☐ **Acquire Family History**

Evaluate how trauma affected caregiver(s): ______

How do caregivers feel now? How does this compare with how they felt before the trauma?

**Worksheet 3.2**

## Cue-Centered Therapy Assessment Note-Taking Form (Optional)

*Instructions*: Please complete each field when working with the child.

| History of present illness, symptoms, and trauma history | Past psychiatric history |
|---|---|
| Medical history (e.g., medications, diagnoses, major illnesses or surgeries) | Developmental history (e.g., pregnancy, delivery, milestones such as talking, eating, and walking) |
| Family history | Social history (e.g., friends, drugs, gangs, firearms, Child Protective Services/legal involvement) |
| Mental status | Differential diagnoses and other diagnoses |

# ✓ PHASE 1

# CHAPTER 4 Session 1: Education

*This session should be conducted with the youth and the caregiver.*

## MATERIALS NEEDED

- Session 1 Review Form
- Thought/Body Feeling/Emotion/Behavior Square
- List of Potential Cues Worksheet
- Toolbox
- Psychoeducational Resources for Caregivers
  - National Institute of Mental Health (NIMH)—Helping Children and Adolescents Cope with Violence and Disasters: www.nimh.nih.gov/health/publications/helping-children-and-adolescents-cope-with-violence-and-disasters-parents/index.shtml
  - American Academy of Child and Adolescents Psychiatry (AACAP)—Facts for Families (available in different languages): www.aacap.org/AACAP/Families_and_Youth/Facts_for_Families/Home.aspx?hkey=fc8eda98-f824-4988-bb07-d49a8545e4e8

  Refer to the following handouts:

  - *Posttraumatic Stress Disorder*
  - *Child Abuse—The Hidden Bruises*
  - *Child Sexual Abuse & Responding to Child Sexual Abuse*
  - *Helping Children after a Disaster*

- National Child Traumatic Stress Network (NCTSN) (includes resources in Spanish): http://nctsnet.org/resources/audiences/parents-caregivers

## OUTLINE

- Provide general psychoeducation regarding trauma and treatment.
- Introduce CCT, including its general format, concepts, and activities.
- Assign take-home activities and provide caregivers with the relevant resources for further information.

## Session Overview

### Goals

- Disseminate knowledge to the child and caregiver on the psychological aftermath of trauma, the long-term consequences of not addressing the trauma, and the benefits of treatment.
- Provide a conceptualization of trauma and the treatment process. Explain the structure of CCT.

### Therapist's Role

- Communicating information clearly
- Building a rapport and providing hope

## Psychoeducation

The primary goal of session 1 is psychoeducation, which involves educating the youth and his caregiver about the condition with which they present to treatment. For this manual specifically, this means teaching them about trauma, its associated symptoms, and PTSD (see Worksheet 4.1, Session 1 Review Form). Throughout, consider replacing the word *trauma* with the phrases *ongoing stress, chronic trauma*, or even *when bad things happen*. Identify the term that is best suited to the child and caregiver experience.

There are three main points to convey in session 1: normal reactions after trauma, the potential for ongoing or reoccurring problems if left untreated, and the efficacy of treatment.

## Introduction

### Normal Stress Response and Trauma

Explain that, throughout evolution, our body has learned to manage stressors by adapting physiologically and psychologically. Trauma prompts the body's normal reaction to stress to become highly responsive. When a child experiences trauma, the feelings, thoughts, and behaviors that follow result from this susceptibility. This is not an abnormal, unusual, "crazy," or "weird" process. If we are crossing the street, for example, and a speeding truck approaches us, our body responds by jumping out of the way. Trauma sometimes can feel as if we were experiencing this level of threat on an ongoing basis. To afford protection, the normal stress response is on the alert. It prepares and launches even in situations that are not threatening. It is this sensitization to the stress response that we call *posttraumatic stress disorder*, or *PTSD*.

### Necessity of Treatment

Emphasize to both caregiver and child the need for treatment to get relieve from PTSD symptoms. This sensitization of the fear or threat system does not heal automatically. The symptoms of PTSD may exacerbate if we do not address them; PTSD feeds on avoidance. Trauma in childhood, if left untreated, can have multiple effects in adolescence and adulthood, ranging from substance abuse to self-harm and physical health problems. Convey that despite the negative outcomes of trauma, posttraumatic symptoms are responsive to psychotherapy, and treatment can help the child resume his earlier functioning.

### Child and Caregiver Perspectives

The child and caregiver may develop ideas regarding which experiences anticipated the symptoms. Inquire about these and explore them. It is crucial for the child to understand he is not at fault for the events that led to the symptoms. Education on the nature of trauma and its effects provides the caregiver with an alternative construct to understand their child's condition. Without this information, caregivers may tend to blame themselves or see themselves as unfitting caregivers. Even worse, caregivers may feel that posttraumatic behaviors and symptoms result from "acting out" or reflect the temperament of the child. Education has the effect of decreasing caregivers' anxiety and making them more open to helping the child. Academic, social, and emotional ramifications of PTSD should be discussed. Here is a case example:

*A Vietnamese immigrant, Hanh, presented to treatment with her son, Duong, because of her inability to manage his violent and angry outbursts toward his siblings. Hanh's husband, Duong's father, had been physically abusive toward the family, and Hanh had reported this domestic violence to the police, resulting in the father's deportation. Hanh feels that Duong is hitting his siblings to aggravate her because of his resentment toward her for getting rid of his dad. When Hanh comes to realize, through psychoeducation, that her son is experiencing posttraumatic symptoms, she decreases her own guilt and negative cognitions about his behavior. This makes her less anxious and more available to her son. Feeling more support from his mother, Duong starts working on improving his behavior.*

## Introduction to Cue-Centered Therapy

During this session, introduce general aspects of CCT—mainly, its structure and activities. Explain the general format of therapy and give an overview of the four phases of this therapy (psychoeducation and coping skills, life story, cue identification and exposure, and a revisit of the life story with the new tools, followed by the conclusion of therapy).

### Thought/Body Feeling/Emotion/Behavior Square

Using the Thought/Body Feeling/Emotion/Behavior Square (Worksheet 4.2), explain how trauma can cause effects in four core areas—cognition, physiology, emotional feeling, and behavior—and how CCT was developed to address each of these areas. For example, starting in the upper left corner of Worksheet 4.2 (THOUGHT), mention that changing a thought may have the impact of changing all the other three corners, resulting in a new response. Begin empowerment and self-efficacy work by letting the child know that he has the power to change a thought; you may want to request a thought from the child that has been bothering him, and demonstrate how the thought can be changed. Use this process for the other three corners.

Introduce the term *cues* and explain how cues relate to behavioral responses. Cues trigger behavioral responses; although these responses may seem automatic, we can alter this connection. Reference the Thought/Body Feeling/Emotion/Behavior Square to explain that cues may lead to responses that are characterized by these four components.

### Cues and Conditioning

The psychoeducational process also involves a brief overview of the main therapeutic concepts:

1. Past traumatic events come to be associated with formerly neutral objects and occurrences. These formerly neutral stimuli (cues) become associated with a sense of fear.
2. The cues then evoke a sense of anxiety and threat even when there is no danger. This sense of threat evokes fear-related behavioral responses.
3. Cues are mostly neutral, not positive or negative. Their negative association is the result of conditioning. In the case of domestic violence exposure, family members may be cues to each other. If both a child and a mother are survivors of a father's violence, for example, the child can be a cue for the mother and vice versa.
4. Learning mindfulness, relaxation, and coping strategies can help decrease stress and posttraumatic reactions.
5. Recounting the history of traumatic events can eventually decrease posttraumatic symptoms through the process of narrative exposure. Similarly, confronting feared cues can help reduce an ongoing feeling of fear or threat.

### Confrontation of Traumatic History and Cues

Let the youth know that a critical part of treatment is to confront the traumatic history and traumatic reminders. Acknowledge that this can appear daunting (or scary) at first, but that it will eventually help him manage his current difficulties. Sharing scenarios similar to the following may facilitate this point:

*Think about what happens if you break your arm. The initial break is really awful, painful, and scary, but then it is over and you go home. Your caregiver sees your broken arm and takes you to the hospital so the doctor can fix your arm. At the hospital, the doctor has to set your arm, which hurts again, but this process is necessary so your arm can heal correctly and regain its strength, and the reset of the broken bone does not hurt as much as the original break. CCT is similar to this process. We will confront painful, bad experiences, and at times it may hurt, but we need to do that to help you heal and grow.*

### Introduction to Take-Home Activities

Stress how much of the work required occurs outside of the sessions through practice on what is learned during sessions. Although the caregiver does not need to return until mid therapy (session 8), encourage the caregiver to be a coach in helping to identify cues and responses to those cues. Explain that take-home activities facilitate the child's practice outside the sessions, and the caregiver provides coaching. These activities reinforce and build on lessons learned in therapy, and allow generalization to the child's everyday life. Note that the youth and the caregiver must complete the take-home activities diligently to gain maximum benefits. Do not use the word *homework* when referring to take-home activities; this may have a negative connotation. Take-home activities are opportunities to practice and build mastery; they are no assignments that are graded. Use positive reinforcement and encouragement throughout therapy to maintain the child's engagement in take-home activities.

In families with intergenerational trauma, a sense of hopelessness may be pervasive. For the youth and his caregiver to engage in treatment, they must feel and understand that the therapist believes in the treatment he is offering; the therapist's enthusiasm and dedication to the therapy can lay the foundation for this sense of hope. The Toolbox (Worksheet 4.3) and the concept of take-home activities are concrete strategies of the treatment that help provide hope and a sense of self-efficacy. The List of Potential Cues (Worksheet 4.4) may play a similar role for caregivers, stressing the importance of their role in therapy. The Toolbox and take-home activities both underscore the role of the youth and the caregiver as active participants and collaborators in treatment, rather than passive recipients.

## Take-Home Activities

- ✐ Based on their observations during the coming weeks, have the caregiver and the child fill out the List of Potential Cues (Worksheet 4.4). The caregiver should bring the form to session 8. Not all cues will be identified; rather, some specific cues will be used for therapeutic training. The goal is for the child to be able to generalize the lessons learned to other cues.
- ✐ Provide the child with the Toolbox (Worksheet 4.3), to be added to throughout therapy.
- ✐ Provide the caregiver with the NIMH, AACAP, and NCTSN handouts as appropriate.

## Session 1 Review Form

*Instructions*: Please complete after session.

☐ **Provide Education**

- ☐ Posttraumatic symptoms as a sensitization of the normal fear response
- ☐ Long-term nature of posttraumatic symptoms
- ☐ Efficacy of treatment

☐ **Provide Literature Resources**

- ☐ NIMH, AACAP, and NCTSN handouts to caregiver

☐ **Provide List of Potential Cues Worksheet**

- ☐ Presented and described to caregiver

☐ **Provide Toolbox**

- ☐ Presented and described to child

☐ **Provide Thought/Body Feeling/Emotion/Behavior Square**

- ☐ Presented and described to child

□ Detail Progress Notes

## Worksheet 4.2

### Thought/Body Feeling/Emotion/Behavior Square

*Instructions*: Use figure to illustrate.

All our reactions have four main components. These components influence each other.

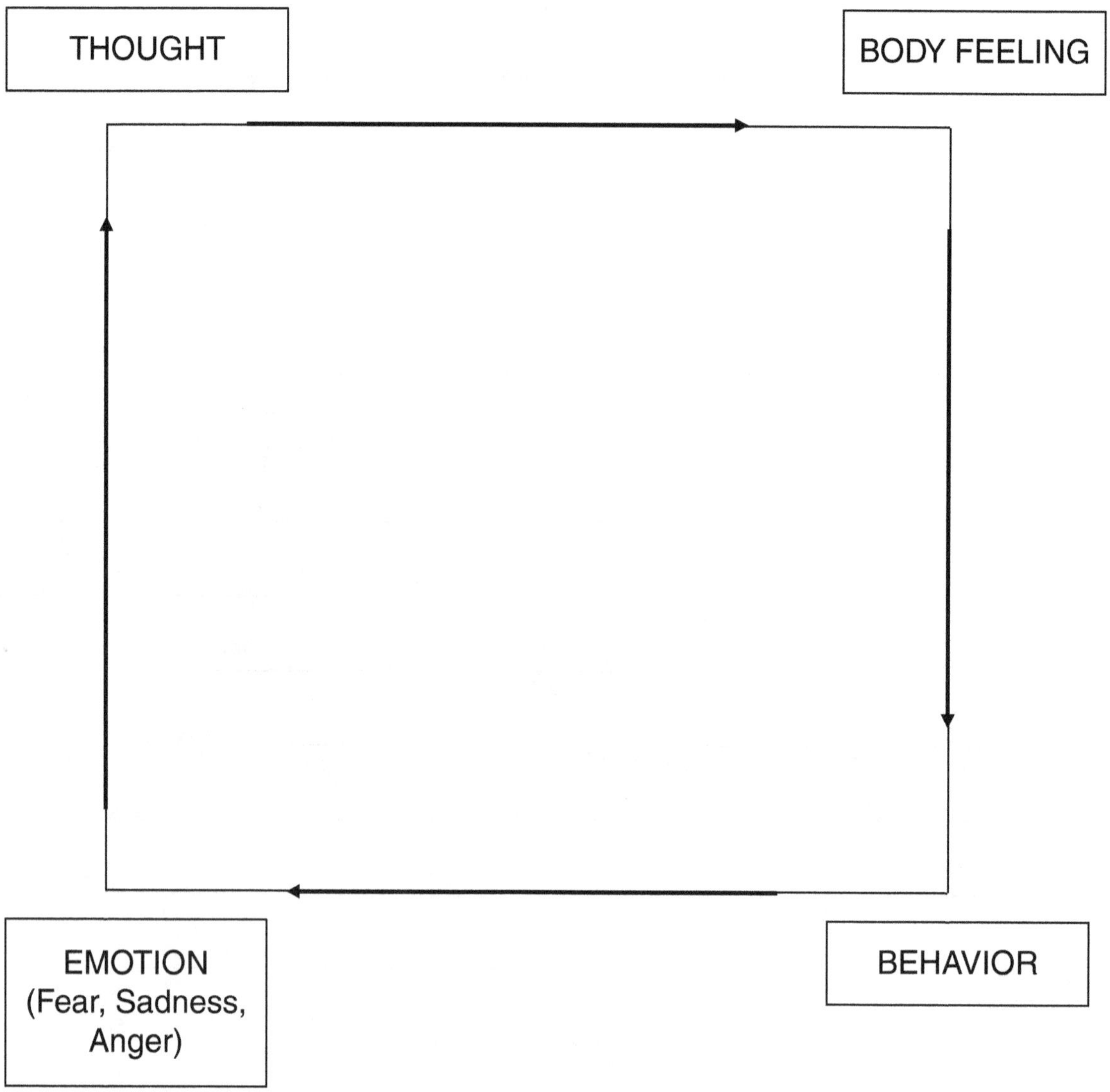

## Toolbox

*Instructions*: Write in helpful tools.

A tool is anything that you can think of or do that helps you develop a new reaction for your cues. As we learn about tools together, you add the ones you like to your Toolbox.

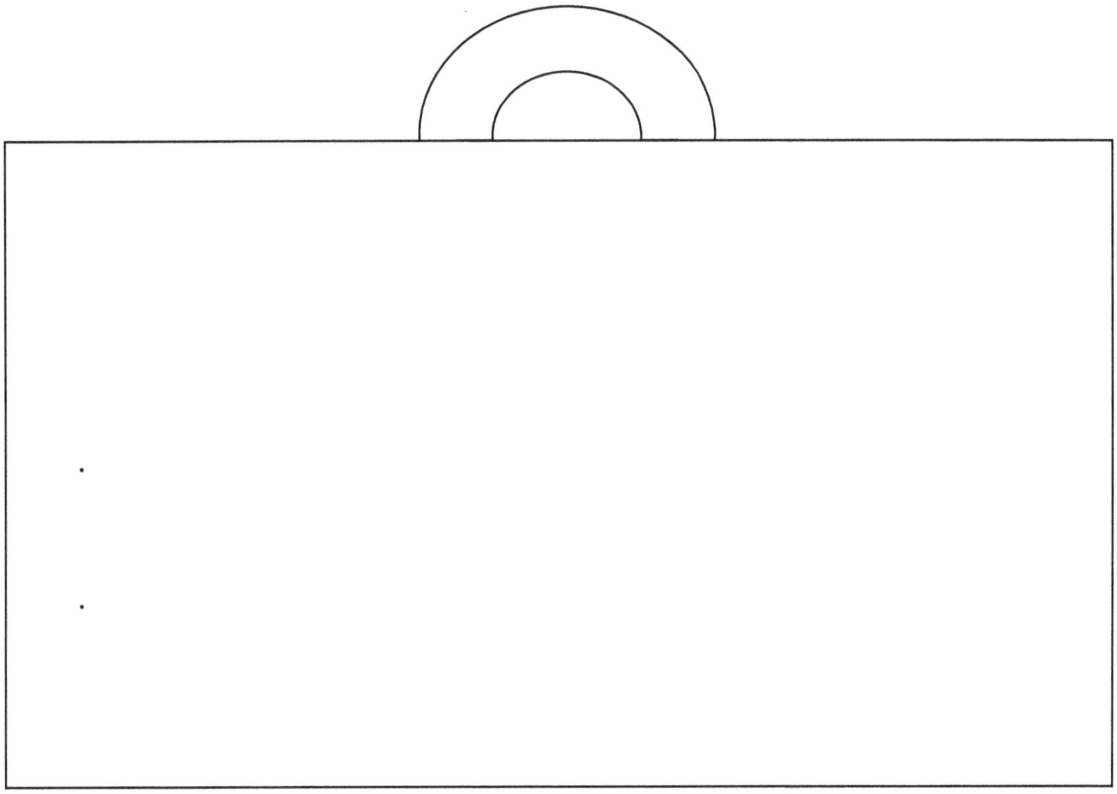

## List of Potential Cues

*Instructions*: Caregiver please write in potential cues. Your child may suggest some cues.

A cue is not necessarily something good or bad; it's just there. It can be anything—a smell, a color, a person, a situation, or anything else—that prompts thoughts or emotions of the traumatic event or events. You may not be aware of the connection between the cue and the response. The caregiver must bring this form to the midtherapy update session (session 8).

*Please list anything that may be acting as a cue:*

1.
2.
3.
4.
5.
6.
7.
8.
9.
10.
11.
12.
13.
14.
15.

# CHAPTER 5 Sessions 2 and 3: Mindfulness, Relaxation, and Cognitive Tools

*This session should be conducted with the child.*

## MATERIALS NEEDED

- Therapist Forms
    - Thought Insertion Model
    - Session 2 Review Form
    - Session 3 Review Form
- Youth Forms
    - Toolbox
    - The Feelings Thermometer
    - Positive Thoughts Worksheet
    - Thought Insertion Worksheet
- Raisins or other pieces of fruit the child enjoys to complete the mindfulness exercise

## OUTLINE

- Introduce the concept of tools.
- Teach the youth behavioral relaxation techniques, including progressive muscle relaxation and deep breathing, and introduce The Feelings Thermometer.

- Guide the youth through the visual imagery exercise.
- Teach the concept of mindfulness.
- Instruct the child on how to apply cognitive techniques such as recruiting positive thoughts and using thought insertion techniques.
- Encourage the youth to develop her own tools.
- Continue teaching and practicing skills during session 3.
- Assign take-home activities.

## Sessions Overview

During sessions 2 and 3, the therapist and child counteract the effects of adverse life events and chronic traumatic stress by focusing on three areas:

1. Management of physiological symptoms related to fear, anxiety, and threat
2. Emotional awareness and control over emotions
3. Cognitive restructuring to help manage intrusive, pervasive, and negative thoughts

In addition to their protective role during the upcoming narrative exposure, these new skills help the child identify her bodily sensations, thoughts, and emotions, and—through this awareness—help her gain mastery and control over her reactions.

Two sessions are devoted to developing this skill set to reinforce the importance of practice and rehearsal. Session 2 consists of training in the application of the tools whereas session 3 is devoted to practicing the new skills. As with any skill, with practice, tool use becomes more natural and is thus more readily available during stressful situations. Using the example of a skill the youth has learned, such as swimming, best illustrates the importance of rehearsal. Having the child practice tool use outside of therapy during stressful everyday-life situations encourages skill mastery and generalization.

### Goal

- Teach the child exercises that will help her acquire mindfulness, relaxation, and cognitive skills. These exercises are useful during examination of the life timeline in the upcoming chronic traumatic stress history sessions (sessions 4 and 5), during completion of take-home activities, and later during the exposure sessions.

### Therapist's Role

- Teaching skills and highlighting the importance of practice (These skills should be practiced daily by the child; eventually, they may become automatic responses.)
- Encouraging the child to develop her own tools

## Introduction to Tools

At the beginning of session 2 reintroduce the youth to the concept of tools, which was first mentioned during session 1. Use the Session 2 Review Form (Worksheet 5.1) to ensure you cover all topics during this session. Redisplay the Toolbox (Chapter 4, Worksheet 4.3) and invite the child to add tools to the worksheet as she learns them. Eventually, she will include in her Toolbox only those tools she chooses and that she finds most helpful. Inform her that these tools will help her become more aware of her emotions, thoughts, and bodily sensations, and that these tools will also help her in regulating or controlling these emotions, thoughts, and bodily sensations. Tell the child that, initially, the tools included in her own personal Toolbox include those the therapist teaches and, later, those she develops.

Tools will be helpful to manage heightened emotional reactions during and after treatment. An example of a heightened emotion is fear, often characterized by a fight-or-flight response. Here is a sample script to describe the fight-or-flight reaction and introduce the idea of developing tools:

*During this therapy you are going to learn some important skills that may make you feel stronger and more capable of managing difficult situations.*

*Have you ever started to cross the street and then suddenly there was a car coming at you and you jumped back on the curb just in time? Do you remember how it felt? It probably took you a while to calm down afterward. Well, here's what happened in your body at that time. Your brain sensed the danger and rapidly fired off a chemical message to your bloodstream. Your heart reacted instantly with a mighty contraction and pumped a huge, extra burst of blood to your arms and legs. This is part of our ancient cave-time reactions. If a saber-toothed tiger was coming at you, you would have needed the blood in your legs to run as fast as you could, or the blood in your arms to fight off the tiger.*

*So, when you jumped back on the curb, not only did all the physical things happen to your body, but also your body diverted blood from your digestive system. After this took place, you might have felt sick to your stomach.*

*When the brain fires off that first chemical message, it continues to do so as long as it senses danger. It takes anywhere from 15 minutes to more than an hour for the body to return to its normal state. In a true emergency, your body's ability to react this way can keep you alive. It's a wonderful thing that our bodies can do this.*

*However, when a person experiences chronic traumatic experiences, sometimes this reaction happens in greater or lesser degrees even when there isn't a real danger in the environment. Our bodies may react to cues in the environment and may interpret them as dangerous; sometimes we are startled, even when a situation is not dangerous.*

*So here's the most important thing to know. You can stop this flight-or-fight reaction in its tracks by using tools. For example, use long, slow, deep breathing. Your body cannot have a fight-or-flight reaction while you are taking long, slow, deep breaths. You shouldn't breathe like this* [huff and puff quickly], *because that only makes the situation worse. But when you breathe like this* [demonstrate taking long, slow, deep breaths], *you are controlling your body's reaction. You may still have some reaction, because your brain has already fired off the chemical message, but you can stop it from doing anything further, and you decrease the amount of time you feel the anxiety reaction.*

## Relaxation Exercises

The introduction of deep breathing and progressive muscle relaxation should be accompanied by an explanation of the bodily sensations associated with fear (such as rapid heartbeat, hyperventilation, sweaty palms, clenched muscles, and so on), with a particular focus on the youth's individual fear response. Simple awareness and labeling of such physiological processes can provide relief to the child. In some cases, the physiological reaction can be the first indicator of fear, and thus is a signal of distress or a *cue*. Breathing and muscle relaxation exercises enable awareness and promote control over the fear response. Explain to the child that fear and stress are often experienced in the body, and that tools can help control these bodily sensations.

### Deep Breathing

Here is a sample script for teaching slow, deep breathing:

> *We're going to breathe together. We're going to breathe in a large breath, while my finger goes up a mountain, but slowly. Then we're going to breathe out slowly while my finger comes back down the mountain. We'll do this three times. Then, after that, you can indicate with your finger how we go up and down the mountain, and I'll follow you, and we'll do this three more times. Breathe in slowly through your nose* [say this while your index finger completes the first leg of an inverted V suspended in the air between you and the child] *now breathe out slowly through your mouth, as if you were breathing out through a straw* [say this while your index finger comes down the second leg of the inverted V].

Repeat this breathing process two more times and then let the child conduct the exercise three more times.

After practicing the breathing, have the child monitor her body to determine whether there are any changes. You can share how, for many people, these exercises are calming, but for others it may not disrupt anxiety. Have the child write this exercise on her Toolbox if he finds the exercise helpful. Use The Feelings Thermometer (discussed later in this chapter) to monitor feelings before and after exercises.

### Progressive Muscle Relaxation

With progressive muscle relaxation, we teach the child the difference between feeling tense and feeling relaxed. Walk the child through relaxing the major muscle groups (feet, legs, trunk, chest/arms, shoulders, and head), with the child tensing each muscle group and holding it for about 10 seconds, and then letting it go (relaxing).

Repeat each muscle group three times, working up the body beginning at the feet and continuing up to the head. Here is a sample script you might use to teach progressive muscle relaxation:

*We're going to work on teaching you and your body how it feels to be relaxed and how it feels to be tense. Sometimes, we are not aware of how these feel. When you feel anxious or scared, but you don't want to feel that way, progressive muscle relaxation can help your body calm down and become relaxed. Before we begin, get comfortable in your chair with your hands gently resting on your lap and your feet flat on the floor. You may wish to close your eyes as we do these exercises.*

***Feet***

*Lifting your legs slightly, point your toes like a dancer and hold them really hard, as if they cannot bend. Do this while I slowly count . . . 1 . . . 2 . . . 3. Okay, now place your feet back on the floor. Now your feet feel relaxed. Let's repeat this two more times.*

***Legs***

*Lift your legs and hold them out in front of you; make them rigid and hard as a rock. 1 . . . 2 . . . 3 . . . now relax. Now your legs feel relaxed. Let's do that two more times.*

***Stomach***

*Next, pull your stomach in as hard as you can and hold it . . . 1 . . . 2 . . . 3. Now release your muscles. Your stomach feels relaxed. Let's do this two more times.*

***Arms/Chest***

*Pretend that you are going to pick up an orange in each hand to make juice. Now I want you to squeeze your hands, arms, and chest really hard to get all the juice out of those oranges . . . 1 . . . 2 . . . 3. Now let your hands drop loosely at your sides. Now your hands, arms, and chest are relaxed. Let's do this two more times.*

***Shoulders***

*Lift your shoulders up until they can almost touch your ears. Hold it . . . 1 . . . 2 . . . 3, then drop them. Now your shoulders are relaxed. Let's do that two more times.*

***Back***

*Reach both hands straight out in front of you, overlapping your hands. Keeping them straight, lift them over the top of your head. Now bring them behind you, looking at them with your head, so that your arms, head, and back are draped over the back of your chair. Try to look at the wall behind you while your head is upside down. Hold it for 1 . . . 2 . . . 3. Now, bring your arms to the front of you. Now your back is relaxed. Let's do this again two more times.*

#### *Jaw*

*Make the biggest smile you can, trying to get the corners of your mouth to touch your ears. Hold it for 1 . . . 2 . . . 3, then go back to your regular smile. Now your jaw is relaxed. Let's do that again two more times.*

#### *Face*

*We are going to scrunch up our face, like we've tasted something really sour, or smelled something awful, and we'll purse out our lips. Hold it for 1 . . . 2 . . . 3, then let these muscles go. Now your face is relaxed. Let's do that two more times.*

Encourage the child to practice progressive muscle relaxation every night before he goes to sleep.

## The Feelings Thermometer

Through the use of The Feelings Thermometer (Worksheet 5.2), you can monitor the intensity of a given emotion and adjust the intervention accordingly. This tool also facilitates the youth's emotional awareness and provides the child with a sense of control over by increasing awareness on the level of emotion experienced. As with the relaxation tools, also encourage using The Feelings Thermometer outside the sessions.

Introduce The Feelings Thermometer to monitor feelings before and after exercises. Explain to the youth that she will be using this tool to assess her emotional state during the life timeline story of positive, neutral, and negative life events, and that she can also use it to track her own emotions in her everyday life. Note that you will also use the thermometer to gauge her emotional level during therapy.

## Visual Imagery

Visual imagery contributes to relaxation and provides relief from negative thoughts and emotions. Learning that positive imagery can be generated may be particularly helpful with symptoms of reexperience, such as intrusive thoughts.

Here is a sample script to teach visual imagery. Feel free to elaborate on the basic imagery exercise if this seems helpful to the child.

*Sit comfortably. Put both feet flat on the floor and place your hands loose on your lap. Close your eyes and take a nice deep breath and begin to breathe in a relaxed, easy way. Now imagine you are in a place you like. It feels very good being there. Look around you and try to really see this place. Describe it to yourself. Maybe it's sunny; maybe the moon is out. Perhaps there's some water that you can touch. Perhaps there are friendly animals or flowers. You feel good here, relaxed. It is a private place, you don't need to tell me what or where it is.*

*I'm going to be quiet for a minute so you can explore and simply enjoy being in this special place. This is* your *special place. You can think of this place anytime you want to feel better. It is always there for you. Now when you are ready, you can open your eyes.*

If the child has trouble finding an imaginary place, vary this exercise by asking her what places she enjoys—for example, the ocean—then describe the scene, with the waves lapping peacefully, seagulls flying overhead, dolphins jumping, the sand feeling warm between her toes, and so on.

## Mindful Awareness

The relaxation and visual imagery exercises build a foundation for mindful awareness. These skills teach that the body and mental images are interconnected with emotional states. Through these skills, the child learns to recognize the current moment experience. For example, the child may be able to identify and verbalize an emotion (such as anger) when feeling the physical sensation (such as an increased heart rate). The child may learn, for example, that her anger manifests in tightness and tension in her body. She is trained to use mindfulness skills to move toward or into the anger, rather than resisting it or reacting in a maladaptive manner. The child is then trained to pause and practice a few mindful breaths, or to do a simple yoga pose, while feeling the anger. After taking the mindful pause, the child then checks back into her emotional states and observes how the mindfulness practice may have shifted the experience of anger. It is common for children to report that simple mindfulness practices, such as breathing, help them feel calm, happy, and relaxed. Children may include mindful breathing or the name of their favorite yoga poses in their Toolbox as a resource they can use to help them cope with stressful experiences.

### Introduction to Mindfulness

Participate in the activity with the child to normalize the experience, which may seem a bit strange at first. Sitting next to the child, take hold of a raisin (or other food) and follow the prompts below.

Explore the raisin in the following ways:

- **Touch**: How does the raisin feel when you touch it?
- **Smell**: How does the raisin smell if you hold it close to your nose?
- **Sight**: What colors do you see in the raisin and what does the texture look like?
- **Sound**: If you hold the raisin between your fingers and bring it close to your ear, what do you hear as you roll it between your fingers?
- **Taste**: What does it feel like when you put the raisin between your lips? Roll the raisin around in your mouth. What do you sense? Bite into the raisin slowly. What do you taste? What is the sensory experience of slowly chewing and eating the raisin bite by bite?

Take a few minutes to process the experience and reflect on the potential benefits of this practice for the child. Ask her to reflect and tell a story about the experience. Coach the child to verbalize the thoughts, emotions, and sensations she had during the exercise.

### Standing Meditation Practice: Standing like a Mountain

Tell the child to practice the standing meditation practice safely. If the posture does not feel good, she should not perform it. Find a location where the child feels safe and there is enough space available.

The mountain pose can be held for about seven breath cycles or longer. This is also an ideal pose to practice throughout the day—for example, when standing in line, waiting for the bus, right before bed, or first thing in the morning.

Pose instructions:

1. Place your feet together or a hip-width distance apart.
2. Make your spine long.

3. Lift your sternum, or breast bone.
4. Make sure your chin is parallel to the ground.
5. Imagine the crown of your head is lifting—for example, ask the child to picture a helium balloon that is gently lifting her head up.
6. Press down through the balls of the feet and lift the toes up in the shoes and notice how that action increases sensation in the legs.

When the child is in the posture, ask her to tell you about a mountain. What do mountains look like? Do they move? Do they make noise? How strong are they? Encourage the child to process and narrate the experience in terms of emotions, thoughts, and sensations.

## Cognitive Techniques

Positive thoughts and thought insertion techniques begin to address the youth's automatic negative thoughts. The term *automatic thoughts* refers to the individual explanations tied to the negative emotions. These thoughts occur spontaneously and are not well processed or thought out. Because of this lack of processing, people often accept these thoughts as truth. Automatic thoughts generally have their basis in a person's deeper underlying beliefs and assumptions about herself and the world.

Negative automatic thoughts are self- generating. They lead to further negative thinking and, in this way, create a chain that becomes self-sustaining—a cycle of negativity. These negative thought chains are associated with depression and anxiety. Inserting positive thoughts, which are not automatic and require conscious effort, can facilitate disruption of the chain. Both the thought insertion technique and the positive thoughts technique facilitate increased awareness of the unconscious automatic thoughts cycle.

### Positive Thoughts and Thought Insertion Techniques

Instruct the child on how to use cognitive techniques such as recruiting positive thoughts and thought insertion techniques. The Thought Insertion Model (Worksheet 5.3), the Thought Insertion Worksheet (Worksheet 5.4), and the Positive Thought Worksheet (Worksheet 5.5) help facilitate the practice.

Have the youth practice both positive thought and thought insertion anchoring on a negative event from the previous week. Note that the event does not need to be traumatic. Practicing replacing negative thoughts with positive ones in therapy can help the child develop the ability to develop her own positive thoughts in the future.

### Note on Negative Thoughts

While encouraging new thinking and more control over feelings, caution the child that this does not mean that negative thoughts and images must always be shut down or avoided. Negative cognitions and emotions are normative and serve a real purpose. The feelings of fear, sadness, and anger often serve as indicators of real danger and harm in a person's environment. It is natural and healthy to feel afraid when in a threatening situation or to grieve a genuine loss. The tools are designed to help youths cope in situations in which the emotions or thoughts are interfering with their functioning. Tools may help manage emotions that have become so pervasive they hamper the ability to experience positive situations.

## Development of Personal Tools

Children that are engaged in treatment may develop their own tools. This is a good prognostic sign. In our experience, the use of these tools leads to even better outcomes. These tools may be activities such as sports or art. If the youth is not involved currently in any such activities, you might encourage her to pursue an activity she might enjoy. For children who associate arousal states with negative emotions, the arousal of exercise and sports can create more positive associations, which make this sensation more tolerable. Here is an example of personal tool development:

*Ava, a sexual abuse survivor, often experienced panic and an overwhelming fear of being attacked while in the shower. She shared with her therapist that singing sometimes calmed her down and made her feel better. The therapist encouraged Ava to sing aloud or under her breath in situations in which she experienced trauma-related fears. The tool worked to help Ava relax. Listening to music and singing became a powerful tool for Ava to express emotions and cope with traumatic symptoms during the course of therapy.*

Help youths generate a list of their own relaxation tools, including activities such as writing, painting, drawing, acting, exercising, doing sports, playing music, or swimming. These tools can be based on preexisting hobbies or interests, or those that are newly developed.

## Session 3

Continue to teach tools as necessary during session 3. Session 3 is devoted primarily to practicing the skills learned in the prior session (Worksheet 5.6).

### Continued Practice

Practice all new skills and encourage the youth to practice them at home between sessions. Emphasize to the child that, just as any other skill, tools get better with practice. For example, ask, "If I gave you a guitar and had you play me a song right now, how would that go? What about if I had you take lessons for a few months and then you played me a song?" You may also ask her for an example from her own life of something she had to practice to do well.

### Selecting Skills for the Toolbox

After practicing all the skills, have the child determine which tools she wants to maintain in her Toolbox. Evaluate how well each tool fits the youth's strengths. If a particular tool seems too difficult to understand or practice, it may not need to be included in the child's Toolbox.

At the end of session 3, remind the youth that she will begin applying these tools in the next session as she begins to discuss her life events.

## Take-Home Activities

Have the youth practice skills between sessions, including the following:

- Deep breathing
- Progressive muscle relaxation

- Visual imagery
- Mindfulness (e.g., breathing, yoga poses)
- Positive thought and thought insertion techniques

✎ Encourage the youth to develop her own relaxation tools (e.g., sports, music)

**Worksheet 5.1**

## Session 2 Review Form

*Instructions*: Please complete after session.

☐ **Provide Education, Modeling, and Training (Coaching) in How to Use the Following Tools:**

- ☐ Deep-breathing exercise
- ☐ Progressive muscle relaxation
- ☐ The Feelings Thermometer
- ☐ Visual imagery (special-place technique)
- ☐ Introduction to mindfulness
- ☐ Thought insertion technique
- ☐ Positive thoughts

☐ **Guide Patient to Develop His/Her Own Tools**

- ☐ List specific tools

| ____________________ | ____________________ |
|---|---|
| ____________________ | ____________________ |
| ____________________ | ____________________ |
| ____________________ | ____________________ |
| ____________________ | ____________________ |

☐ **Detail Progress Notes**

## The Feelings Thermometer

*Instructions*: Use this instrument to assess level of emotional state before, during and after exercises, exposure, or whenever you need an emotional level anchor. The instrument facilitates assessing change in emotional level or intensity.

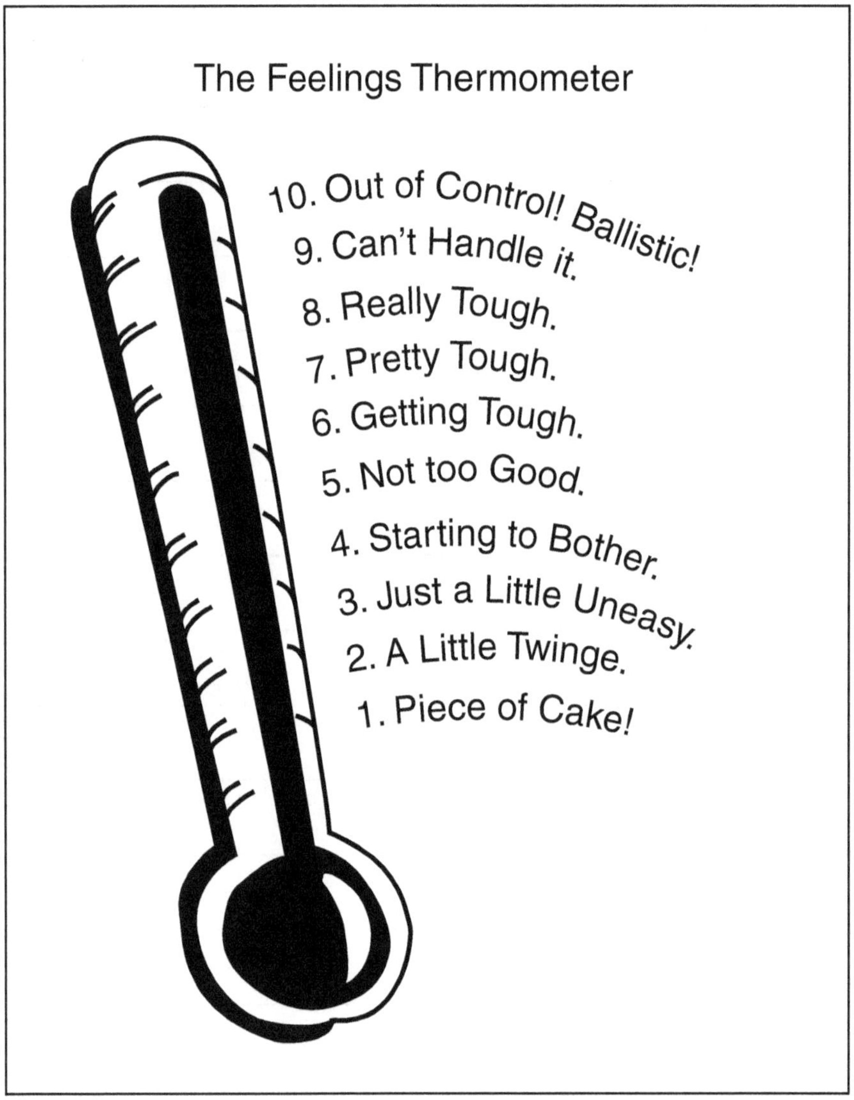

## Thought Insertion Model

*Instructions: Use the following to help the child understand the thought insertion model. Show her the example of the thought insertion technique. Then, go through the Thought Insertion Worksheet (Worksheet 5.4) with her, providing guidance and modeling how to develop positive counterthoughts.*

Negative thoughts can become a cycle, with one negative thought leading to another. You have the power to stop the cycle at any time by inserting positive thoughts.

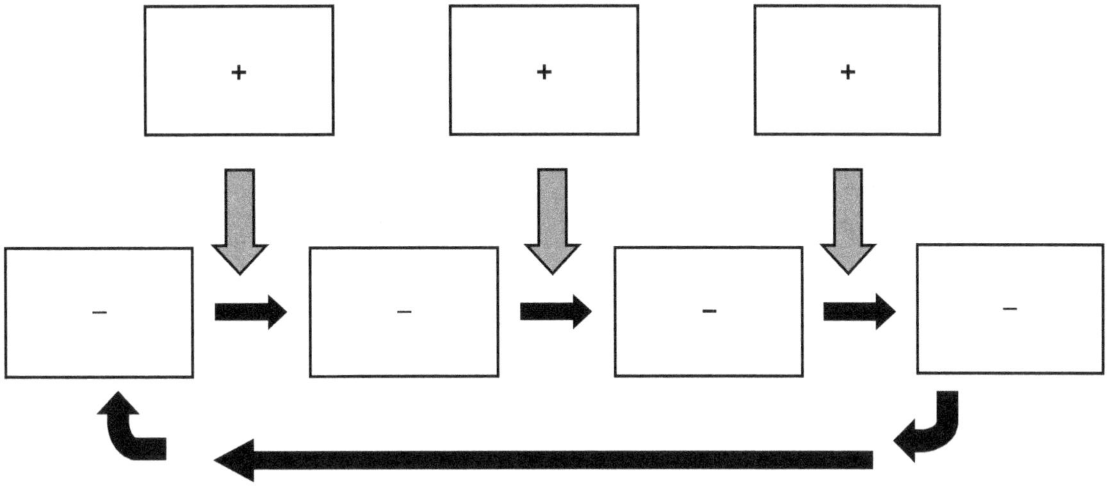


**Example:**

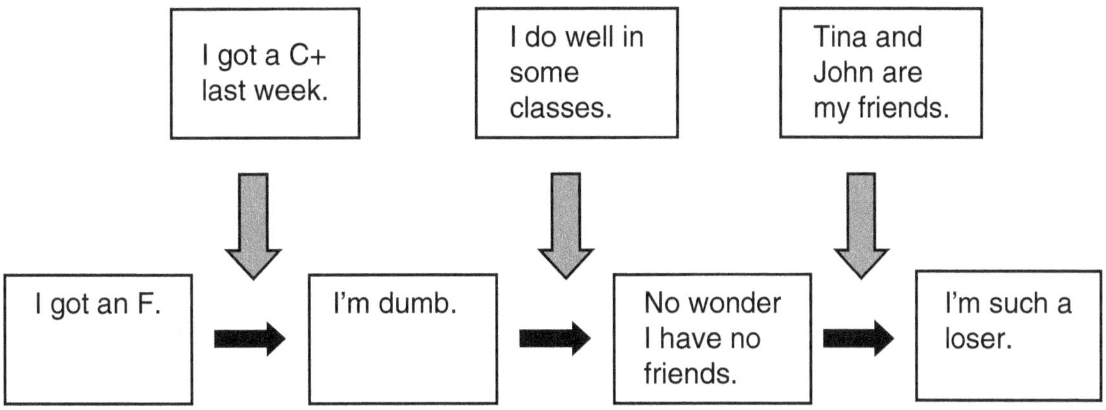

**Worksheet 5.4**

## Thought Insertion Worksheet

*Instructions*: Provide guidance and modeling by developing positive counter thoughts to negative thoughts.

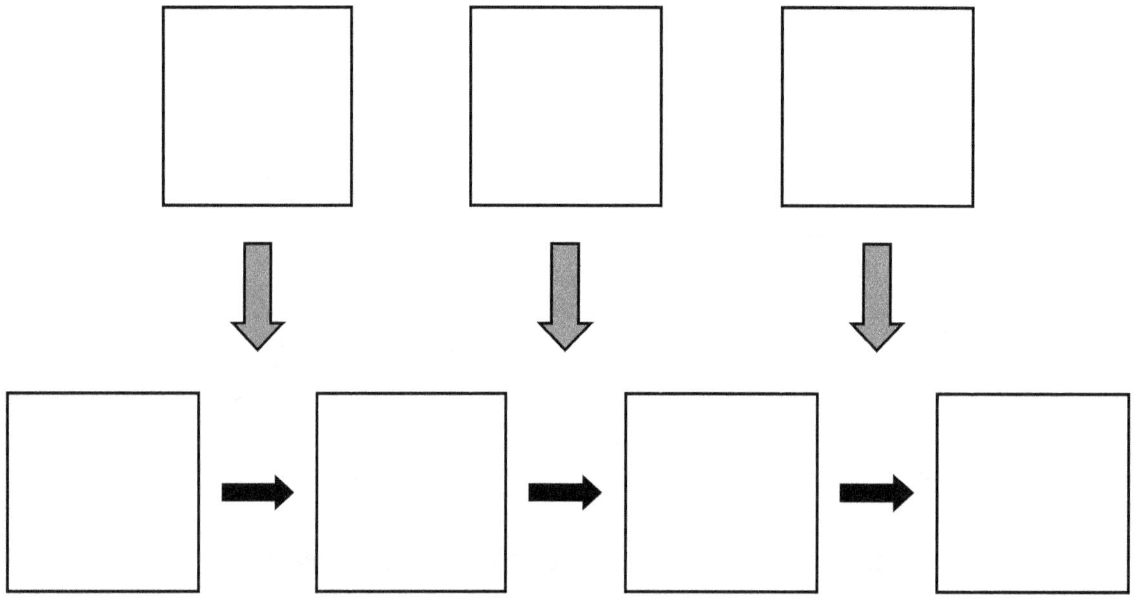

**Worksheet 5.5**

## Positive Thoughts Worksheet

*Instructions:* Think of an upsetting event from the past week and write a description of it. In the negative (–) column, list all the negative thoughts you had about the event and yourself. Come up with positive thoughts that disagree with the negative ones. Try to have at least one more thought in the positive (+) column. For example, if you have three negative thoughts, try to come up with four positive thoughts.

Event: ____________________________________________

____________________________________________

____________________________________________

| – | + |
|---|---|
| **Example:** I got an F on a text. I must be dumb. | But, I also got a C+ this week. |
| | |

## Session 3 Review Form

*Instructions*: For each exercise please keep track of the explanation and the practice. In addition, indicate if it was considered helpful enough to add to the toolbox.

☐ **Indicate Tools Explained (E), Practiced (P), and added to the Toolbox (T)**

- ☐ **E/P/T** Mindfulness practice
- ☐ **E/P/T** Deep-breathing exercise
- ☐ **E/P/T** Progressive muscle relaxation
- ☐ **E/P/T** Visual imagery exercise
- ☐ **E/P/T** The Feelings Thermometer
- ☐ **E/P/T** Positive Thoughts Worksheet
- ☐ **E/P/T** Thought Insertion Model

☐ **Detail Progress Notes**

✓ PHASE 2

# CHAPTER 6 Sessions 4 and 5: Chronic Traumatic Stress History

*This session should be conducted with the child.*

## MATERIALS NEEDED

- Art and play materials (optional)
- Therapist Forms
  - Life Timeline
  - Session 4 Review Form
  - Session 5 Review Form
- Youth Forms
  - Toolbox
  - Feelings worksheets

## OUTLINE

- Review principles of avoidance and exposure therapy as needed.
- Take into account real threats versus cues and note cognitive distortions.
- Explain the parameters of the chronic traumatic stress discussion.
- Complete the life timeline.

- During session 5, continue to explore the life timeline and identify details of events and cues.
- Assign take-home activities.

## Sessions Overview

### Goals

- Assist youths in verbalizing their history of past and ongoing experiences.
- Map events in the child's life and have him rate events as positive, neutral, or negative.
- Model and coach the use of skills and tools learned in prior sessions to manage trauma-related distress.

### Therapist's Role

- Being an active and empathetic listener, and encouraging the youth to begin to verbalize his experiences
- Identifying cognitive distortions within his narrative
- Identifying details of the traumatic events (visual or auditory sensations, spatial and temporal context) that may be acting as cues without the youth's awareness
- Examining the three key emotions of fear, sadness, and anger within the narrative, and helping him explore the content, expression, and context of each emotion

## Principles of Avoidance and Exposure

Provide psychoeducation to the child and caregiver as needed. Before these sessions, review principles of avoidance and exposure therapy as presented below.

### Avoidance

The fear, stress, and anxiety associated with PTSD are maintained through avoidance. Avoidance may first appear as a coping strategy. If the traumatic events are not processed consciously and verbally, avoidance may become the only approach to managing distress from exposure to cues. This defense, however, is porous, and distress may then express itself through symptoms and maladaptive behaviors. If avoidance continues, fear is maintained. Fear can strengthen and become pervasive in the child's life by generalizing to new situations.

### Exposure Therapy

Exposure therapy is an empirically validated treatment that encourages confrontation with the feared object. For elevator phobia, for example, the individual is coached to become exposed gradually to elevators—first by standing in front of one, then by walking in and out of it, then taking the elevator to the first floor, and so on. Exposure during PTSD treatment allows the child to learn that he can confront the feared situations and tolerate them. This new learning enables the youth to uncouple the sensation of fear from the traumatic cues. Because exposure can be a difficult task, the tools in the youth's individualized Toolbox should be used throughout the sessions to help the child manage the fearful, threatening, or anxious feelings associated with the process.

Children who experience ongoing adversity may not have the opportunity to revisit past experiences as they continue to battle current events and work on preventing future ones. This attempt to process experiences taxes the body and decreases its reserve for recuperating. Conscious effort, structured time, and guidance from a caring adult can help revitalize the child's resources.

### Narrative Exposure

The act of telling a life story in therapy, a form of narrative exposure, is not retraumatizing. This exposure allows children to share—in a safe, structured environment and with a caring adult—many of the intrusive thoughts they usually manage on their own. These recurrent intrusive thoughts result, in part, from the failure of avoidance to serve as a defense. Reexperiencing traumatic material may express itself though posttraumatic play, trauma-related dreams, and flashbacks. These symptoms often result in the child experiencing threat in the environment, leading to an ongoing sense of danger and difficulties separating past from present.

Details of the traumatic experience may facilitate identification of cues. Encouraging the child to visualize events and discuss them in the present tense provides increased access to memories. This process increases the effectiveness of exposure while the child tolerates remembering in a safe environment. The child identifies appropriate words to describe the experiences, and associated body feelings and emotions. These words can now be encoded in a new memory.

## Session Notes for the Therapist

While constructing a narrative history with children who have ongoing trauma and adversity, take the following topics into consideration during these sessions: threats and vigilance, and cognitive distortions and compartmentalization.

### Threats and Vigilance

Separating real from perceived threat becomes a more difficult chore for children who live in adversity because, in many instances, their environment may not be safe. It is not the goal of treatment to eliminate vigilance in these children, but to increase their cognitive flexibility. In this manner, they learn to appraise the current situation and become vigilant only if necessary. Vigilance is not maladaptive for these children unless it becomes pervasive and is used without discrimination.

Children who experience ongoing trauma and adversity may continue to face danger or threat. Providing safety measures during therapy helps the chronically traumatized child benefit from the process of exposure. It is important to remind the child about the safeguards and confidentiality practices of therapy. Remember that if a particular situation, event, or occurrence is currently a threat, this is not a cue; it is a threatening situation. Here is a case example:

*Mrs. Johnson brings her son James to therapy because at least once a week she finds him under the bed when she goes to wake him up for school. When asking him about this, the therapist learns that, on occasion, he hears shooting in his neighborhood and he gets under the bed for safety and shelter. The therapist verifies with Mrs. Johnson that shootings occur in this neighborhood.*

In this case scenario, the shooting sounds are not a cue. They are a real threat and James has developed an adaptive response. Therapy may be needed to help him and his mom with current stressors in their living environment, but real threats should not be considered cues.

### Cognitive Distortions and Compartmentalization

Therapists may feel the impetus to begin to correct cognitive distortions during these sessions. Premature interventions may interrupt the narrative. It is important for the child to have the opportunity to continue to communicate how he perceives the events. Refrain from leading comments or questions; open-ended questions are best during these sessions.

Children who experience multiple episodes of violence may live in chaotic environments that are difficult to describe. Attend carefully for words that describe the environment from the child's perspective.

Note any breaks or interruptions as the child relates events, feelings, and emotions. Also note any confusion between past and present in the child's account. This information indicates the level of compartmentalization in the child's mind and the work needed to integrate these components.

During these sessions, assess three key emotions—fear, sadness, and anger—as well as current symptoms and behaviors. Because of children's tendency to compartmentalize, they may not be aware of the interconnectedness of their history, thoughts, feelings, and behaviors. A main goal of these sessions is to help the child link past experiences with current feelings (both physical and emotional), as well as his behaviors. When this is accomplished, it may be easier for the child not to self-blame. Cognitive restructuring during sessions 6 and 7 will support correction of cognitive distortions.

## Discussion Parameters: Chronic Traumatic Stress in Youths

To provide a sense of containment and safety, discuss with the child at the beginning of the session the parameters of the discussion of his chronic traumatic stress—that it will only last a certain number of sessions, that he can use tools as needed to help control his anxiety, and that he chooses what events to discuss.

### Note-taking

Tell the child that that you might take notes during these sessions. Specify that, in most sessions, you will not take notes, but that now it is important to get all the details to understand accurately what has happened in the youth's life.

### Use of the Toolbox

Monitor the child's feelings and encourage using the Toolbox when necessary. There is opportunity to complete work from sessions 2 and 3, but be watchful for avoidance (from the child and/or yourself) to engage on current objectives. The Toolbox and its tools, as well as The Feelings Thermometer, should be available throughout the sessions.

## Life Timeline

A life timeline (Worksheet 6.1) will help guide the discussion and serve as a visual anchor. It may be helpful first to begin the timeline by annotating simple events, such as birthday, first day of school, and so on.

### Importance of Verbalizing Memories

Teach the child the importance of verbalizing emotional memories that previously may have not been encoded with words. It is important to integrate all experiences into a cohesive story; narrating the story of his life begins this process. Explain how this procedure facilitates the connections between the feelings and emotions parts of his brain (the lower brain) and the thinking part of his brain (the upper brain).

Initially, however, encourage the youth to begin to express his story in whatever manner with which he is comfortable, including art, play, and so on. Throughout the course of the sessions, encourage the youth to move from nonverbal to verbal expression. Do not attempt to correct or interpret any of the information; the goal is to gather the story from the child's perspective.

### Guide for Completing Life Timeline

The Life Timeline provides a visual icon that can assist you in keeping track of discussed events and can help the child with recollection of other experiences. Below are some guidelines that facilitate discussion while using the form.

1. Encourage the youth actually to envision the traumatic events in his mind and to remember the thoughts, feelings, and sensations he experienced at the time.
2. Have the child tell the events in the present tense when appropriate. Ask questions that encourage elaboration about details, such as: What do you see? What are your thoughts?
3. Get history and details not only for the traumatic events, but also for the life context in which they are embedded (e.g., when school started, when we moved away). Worksheet 6.1 (the life timeline) can be used to record the youth's history. Have the youth add events in his life to the timeline and have him rate each event as positive, negative, or neutral (neither good nor bad) on a scale of zero to three (zero is neutral, one is a little, two is somewhat, and three is most). Take note of gaps in the youth's memory.
4. Notice the three key emotions (fear, sadness, and anger) as they occur throughout the narrative.
5. At the end of each session, read back to the youth the content he shared. This helps the youth feel heard and understood, and gives him an opportunity to correct any misunderstandings.

## Session 5: Continuation of Life Timeline

Session 5 begins with a discussion of the take-home activity from session 4, getting the child to focus on the emotions. The goal on completion of session 5 is for the child to progress from acknowledging key emotions to linking them to current behaviors (Feelings Worksheets Forms 6.2 and 6.3). The Feelings Worksheet Form 6.4 will further facilitate this process.

Resume completing the life timeline with the child. During further discussion of past and current life events, continue to explore the positive, neutral, and negative experiences and their associated emotions. Ask for clarification about any aspects of the events. Session 5 can be used to identify details of the narrative that are unclear or were not discussed in the previous session. Details often lead to identification of cues.

### Memory Gaps

Note gaps in the child's memory related to the traumatic events and the overall life story. Memory gaps related to traumatic events are a common occurrence among trauma survivors. These gaps may eventually be filled during therapy.

### Potential Cues

Note any potential cues in the child's narrative. These hypothesized cues should be compared with the youth's self-identified cues and the caregiver's List of Potential Cues Worksheet (Chapter 4, Worksheet 4.4).

## Take-Home Activities

- At the end of session 4, assign one of the Feelings worksheets as a take-home activity.
  - If the child seems in touch with the three key emotions, assign Feelings Worksheet Form 6.2.
  - If he does not seem to be able to access his emotions, assign Feelings Worksheet 6.3, which provides more distance from the emotions.
- At the end of Session 5, assign Feelings Worksheet Form 6.4.

**Note**: The Feelings worksheets are designed to facilitate the connections between the chronic traumatic history and emotions (Worksheets 6.3 and 6.4, Feelings 1A and 1B, respectively), and emotions and behaviors (Worksheet 6.5, Feelings 2). The word *feeling* is used rather than *emotion* because this word is more effective with children.

Worksheet 6.1

## Life Timeline

*Instructions: Place key events in the year they happened, rating them from negative 3 (–3) to positive 3 (+3) depending on how the child rates the experience.*

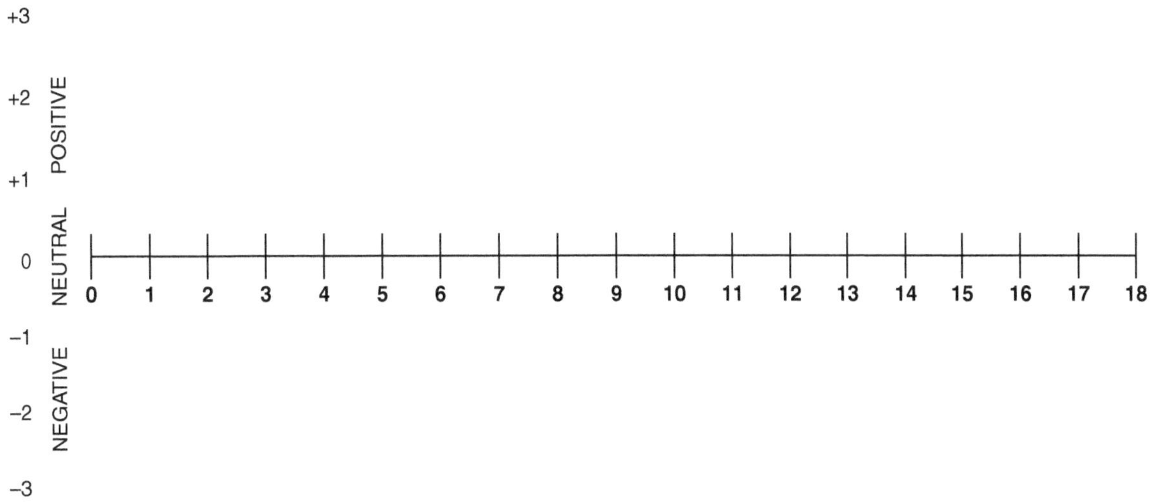

## Feelings 1A Worksheet

*Instructions*: Please complete sentence.

**Because I am FEARFUL (scared, nervous) I**

1.

2.

3.

4.

5.

**Because I am SAD I**

1.

2.

3.

4.

5.

**Because I am ANGRY I**

1.

2.

3.

4.

5.

## Feelings 1B Worksheet

*Instructions*: Please complete sentence.

**If I were FEARFUL (scared, nervous) I would**

1.
2.
3.
4.
5.

**If I were SAD I would**

1.
2.
3.
4.
5.

**If I were ANGRY I would**

1.
2.
3.
4.
5.

## Feelings 2 Worksheet

*Instructions*: Please complete sentence.

**I am FEARFUL (scared, nervous) because**

1.
2.
3.
4.
5.

**I am SAD because**

1.
2.
3.
4.
5.

**I am ANGRY because**

1.
2.
3.
4.
5.

Worksheet 6.5

## Session 4 Review Form

*Instructions*: Please complete after session.

☐ **Summarize Life Timeline**

☐ List Cues Identified

☐ Note Memory Gaps

### ☐ Evaluate Three Key Emotions and Cognitive Distortions Identified in the Chronic Traumatic Stress History

Fear: ______________________________

______________________________

______________________________

______________________________

______________________________

______________________________

______________________________

______________________________

Sadness: ______________________________

______________________________

______________________________

______________________________

______________________________

______________________________

______________________________

______________________________

Anger: ______________________________

______________________________

______________________________

______________________________

Cognitive distortions: ______________________________

☐ **Detail Progress Notes**

**Worksheet 6.6**

## Session 5 Review Form

*Instructions*: Please complete after session.

□ **Identify Cues**

□ **Note Memory Gaps**

☐ **Evaluate Three Key Emotions and Cognitive Distortions Identified in the Chronic Traumatic Stress History**

Fear: ______________________________

______________________________

______________________________

______________________________

______________________________

______________________________

______________________________

______________________________

Sadness: ______________________________

______________________________

______________________________

______________________________

______________________________

______________________________

______________________________

______________________________

Anger: ______________________________

______________________________

______________________________

______________________________

______________________________

______________________________

____________________________________________________

____________________________________________________

Cognitive distortions: ________________________________________

☐ **Detail Progress Notes**

# CHAPTER 7 Sessions 6 and 7: Processing the Chronic Traumatic Stress History

*This session should be conducted with the child.*

## MATERIALS NEEDED

- Therapist Forms
  - Session 6 Review Form
  - Session 7 Review Form
  - Life Timeline
- Youth Forms
  - Feelings Worksheet 6.4
  - The Feelings Thermometer
  - The Toolbox
  - Positive Thoughts Worksheet
  - Thought Insertion Worksheet

## OUTLINE

- Review the Feelings Worksheet 6.4 and complete the life timeline.
- Correct cognitive distortions indicated in the traumatic events narrative.

- Facilitate the identification and labeling of emotions, and integrate them into the life narrative. This is an appropriate time to correct cognitive distortions.
- Restructure the youth's life story to include positive events as well as traumatic events. For traumatic events, help frame the youth as a survivor rather than a victim.
- Assign take-home activities.

## Sessions Overview

The cognitive and supportive therapeutic work in these sessions will challenge youths' misconceptions about the events. The therapist and child should work together to build cognitive flexibility. Cognitive flexibility is the ability to shift thought and response appropriately to a new event or situation. The child becomes empowered by identifying misconceptions and by learning when arousal and vigilance are appropriate, and when it is more adaptive to relax and trust.

The goal of these sessions is not to replace the child's outlook with an overly positive story that her own experience may not warrant. It is to balance the trauma-saturated story, sustained by intrusive negative thoughts, with information and perspectives drawn from the youth's life and strengths.

### Goals

- Empower the child.
- Conduct cognitive restructuring.

### Therapist's Role

- Assisting in verbalizing the key emotions of fear, sadness, anger
- Providing hope
- Correcting cognitive distortions
- Attempting to fill memory gaps without suggestion
- Helping the child incorporate chronic traumatic events into the larger narrative of her life

- Identifying positive areas in the child's life and areas where she exerts control, and including the constructive restructuring of her life story
- Redefining the child's role as a survivor rather than a victim

## Review and Life Timeline

Begin by discussing the Feelings 2 Worksheet (Chapter 6, Worksheet 6.4), assigned during the previous session. Together, incorporate the discussion into the life timeline. Complete rating the events on the life timeline (Worksheet 6.1).

## Correction of Cognitive Distortions

Return to the chronic traumatic events narrative and correct cognitive distortions. Use the Positive Thoughts and Thought Insertion worksheets (Chapter 5, Worksheet 5.5 and Worksheet 5.4, respectively) to facilitate the process (refer back to the introduction of these worksheets in sessions 2 and 3, and photocopy additional sheets as needed).

### Cognitive Distortions

Cognitive distortions are overly rigid. They help develop and maintain negative thoughts and emotions. Children who have undergone chronic traumatic stressors can experience such distortions, including survivor's guilt, self-blame, a belief there is something wrong with them, and a view that the world is a dangerous place. Such distortions result from children's attempts to make sense of overwhelming situations. Youths may be particularly prone to developing distorted ways of thinking, but these distortions can last a lifetime if not addressed.

Note that many negative thoughts associated with traumatic experiences and adversity are not distorted; they are real. These are not the focus of intervention during these sessions. Rather, concentrate on inflexible modes of thinking that involve the role of the child in a negative context.

### Cognitive–Behavioral Techniques

Cognitive–behavioral techniques, such as reframing and reattribution, can be used to correct cognitive distortions. Contradictory evidence can be drawn from the youth's own life timeline. Encourage the child to reexamine her thoughts from a more flexible viewpoint, avoiding rigid categorization and black-and-white thinking. Ask her to clarify general negative terms such as *loser* or *bad*. Note any inflexible rules to which the child may adhere, such as "I should have . . . ." Youth who experience trauma are often empathetic toward others who have suffered; ask the child to apply that same empathy to herself.

The youth's ability to challenge her own thoughts enhances her insight into the effect of the traumatic experiences and her ability to counteract these effects. This process builds self-efficacy and leads to more flexibility and realistic appraisals. The youth's involvement in this process is vital. Children are more likely to accept self-generated statements than those imposed by therapy. If the child can state "I guess it was not my fault" before the therapist volunteers "It wasn't your fault," the gains are more significant.

## Identification of Emotions

Work with the child to identify and label the three key emotions (fear, sadness, and anger) within key events of the life timeline.

### Role of Emotion in Cognitive Restructuring

Emotional exploration is necessary to reinforce cognitive corrections. The change in thinking should be accompanied by an emotional belief. The cognitive distortion may exist as a verbal memory, hence correcting it may not expand to memories that were encoded differently. Referring to the Thought/Body Feeling/Emotion/Behavior Square (Chapter 4, Worksheet 4.2) may assist in generalizing thought changes to the other three components of a response.

Feeling detached or numb may mask other emotions; however, do not force disclosure of emotional states because they may not be accessible to the child. Focus on current emotions and allow their expression during the sessions while identifying words to describe them.

By labeling emotions and linking them to specific experiences related to the traumatic events, you can guide the child in connecting verbal and emotional aspects of the trauma narrative. Highlight the negative events in the life timeline and refer to them as *traumatic history, stressful experiences*, or *adverse childhood experiences*. Encourage the child to apply her own label—for example, "the bad things that happened" or "unfair experiences"—and then use the child's description.

### Individual Expression of Emotions

During sessions 4 and 5, and even with the assistance of the Feelings worksheets, children may respond to their emotions with a simple, "I felt bad." During sessions 6 and 7, encourage the youth to use specific words to describe how she felt. Because the emotions experienced by the child will be unique, these words should come directly from the youth and not from you, the therapist. Remember, offer firm guidance, but no suggestions. For example, instead of saying, "By bad, do you mean sad?" Ask, "What do you mean by bad?" Open-ended questions help elucidate the true feelings and emotions the child needs to express.

## Constructive Restructuring of the Youth's Life Story

Guide the youth toward a complete verbal narrative of her traumatic history. In addition to connecting the trauma-related emotions, thoughts, and memories, the traumatic events should be discussed within the broader story of the child's life. Highlight positive and neutral life events as well as traumatic ones. This strategy strengthens the idea of the youth as survivor rather than a victim.

The fact that the child is working in this therapeutic collaboration makes her a survivor of the events. Reinforce ways in which the child confronted and continues to face the events—being strong, making it through, seeking assistance, telling, caring for others. Help prevent incorporation of the "victim" mind-set into the identity of the young person.

## Take-Home Activities

- ✎ Remind caregivers they are to attend session 8 and bring the List of Potential Cues Worksheet (Chapter 4, Worksheet 4.4).
  **Note**: On the List of Potential Cues Worksheet, caregivers can list any potential cues they think may trigger the child's symptoms. These do not become a cue until agreed to by the child, but they provide a working list. In addition, this activity sensitizes the caregiver to the need to pay attention to the environment.

**Worksheet 7.1**

## Session 6 Review Form

*Instructions*: Please complete after session.

☐ **Restructure Cognitive Distortions in the Trauma Narrative**

Distortion: ______________________________

______________________________

______________________________

Corrective Thought(s): ______________________________

______________________________

______________________________

Distortion: ______________________________

______________________________

______________________________

Corrective Thought(s): ______________________________

______________________________

______________________________

Distortion: ______________________________

______________________________

______________________________

Corrective Thought(s): ______________________________

______________________________

______________________________

Distortion: ______________________________________________

______________________________________________

______________________________________________

Corrective Thought(s): ______________________________________________

______________________________________________

______________________________________________

☐ **Evaluate Three Key Emotions Identified in the Narrative**

Fear: ______________________________________________

______________________________________________

______________________________________________

______________________________________________

______________________________________________

______________________________________________

______________________________________________

______________________________________________

Sadness: ______________________________________________

______________________________________________

______________________________________________

______________________________________________

______________________________________________

______________________________________________

______________________________________________

______________________________________________

Anger: ______________________________

______________________________

______________________________

______________________________

______________________________

______________________________

______________________________

______________________________

☐ **Detail Progress Notes**

______________________________

______________________________

______________________________

______________________________

______________________________

______________________________

______________________________

______________________________

______________________________

______________________________

______________________________

______________________________

______________________________

______________________________

**Worksheet 7.2**

## Session 7 Review Form

*Instructions*: Please complete after session.

☐ **Restructure Cognitive Distortions in Trauma Narrative**

Distortion: ______________________________________________

______________________________________________

______________________________________________

Corrective Thought(s): ______________________________________________

______________________________________________

______________________________________________

Distortion: ______________________________________________

______________________________________________

______________________________________________

Corrective Thought(s): ______________________________________________

______________________________________________

______________________________________________

Distortion: ______________________________________________

______________________________________________

______________________________________________

Corrective Thought(s): ______________________________________________

______________________________________________

______________________________________________

Distortion: ______________________________________________

______________________________________________

______________________________________________

Corrective Thought(s): ______________________________________________

______________________________________________

______________________________________________

☐ **Evaluate Three Key Emotions Identified in the Narrative**

Fear: ______________________________________________

______________________________________________

______________________________________________

______________________________________________

______________________________________________

______________________________________________

______________________________________________

Sadness: ______________________________________________

______________________________________________

______________________________________________

______________________________________________

______________________________________________

Anger: ______

☐ **Detail Progress Notes**

✓ PHASE 3

# CHAPTER 8 Session 8: Midtherapy Update

*This session should be conducted with the youth and the caregiver.*

## MATERIALS NEEDED

- List of Potential Cues Worksheet
- The Feelings Thermometer
- Toolbox
- Session 8 Review Form

## OUTLINE

- Review the List of Potential Cues Worksheet brought by the caregiver.
- Review the youth's progress up to the current session, with the child also relaying information to the caregiver.
- Prepare the caregiver for his involvement in the upcoming exposure work that will take place both during sessions and at home.

### Session Overview

The goals of session 8 are multifaceted. The youth receives validation for his arduous work. He is empowered through positive feedback and by serving as a co-informer on his progress in therapy. Success and self-efficacy counteract feelings of victimization or powerlessness.

### Goals

- The child experiences caregiver engagement in the therapy process.
- The child feels empowered and active in his progress.
- The caregiver understands and considers his key role in the treatment process.
- The child and therapist inform the caregiver about the methods and progress of therapy.

### Therapist's Role

- Informing the caregiver on the therapeutic process
- Providing positive feedback to the child on his work in therapy
- Supporting the child as he updates the caregiver on his therapy's progress
- Preparing the caregiver to act as a facilitator (coach) during the next phase of treatment
- Evaluating clinical progress

## Review of Potential Cues

Session 8 reintroduces the concept of cues to the youth and his caregiver. Use the caregiver's completed List of Potential Cues Worksheet (Chapter 4, Worksheet 4.4) to begin this conversation. The list should include cues suggested by the child as well as your hypothesized cues. This discussion sets the foundation for the exposure phase of treatment.

## Review of Youth's Progress

Discuss work from sessions 1 through 7, with both you and the youth relaying information to the caregiver. During this session, the caregiver may be able to provide information on academic, social, or emotional (e.g., school, peer relations, home) progress since session 1. Objective assessments through the use of questionnaires may be used during this session. Compliment the youth on work he is doing in therapy.

## Caregiver Involvement

The caregiver's presence during session 8 highlights his significance in his child's improvement. The inclusion of the caregiver helps to convey to him that he is involved in the therapeutic process and that he, the therapist, and the youth are all working together as a team to combat the youth's trauma-related issues. Attempt to gauge the caregiver's commitment to the treatment process. An uncommitted caregiver has the potential to undo some of the work completed in therapy.

Emphasize the vital role of the caregiver in supporting and coaching child through the at-home exposure activities. During this session, train caregivers on how to respond to and support the child during the cue exposure phase.

### Preparation for Caregiver Coaching

Through both direct instruction and modeling, prepare the caregiver for his role as a coach during cue exposure in the next sessions. Praising the youth during the session exemplifies to the caregiver how to reinforce the child's progress. Also, educate the caregiver on the various tools in the youth's Toolbox. Instruct the caregiver to encourage the child's practice of tools during stressful situations and during cue exposure.

### Psychoeducation

Psychoeducation continues to be present in all sessions. During this session emphasize to caregiver that avoiding discussion just furthers the maintenance of posttraumatic symptoms. Illustrate how both his child and him are demonstrating an approach style that is beneficial to recovery. When this approach takes the form of exposure to safe cues, it may lead to the extinction of the association between cues and distress, and may result in a more adaptive response.

**Worksheet 8.1**

## Session 8 Review Form

*Instructions:* Please complete after session.

☐ **Discuss Youth's Progress in Therapy and Compliment His/Her Work**

Praises given:

☐ **Collect List of Potential Cues Worksheet and Discuss Potential Cues**

Therapist input on cues list:

Youth input on cues list: ____________________________________________

______________________________________________________________

______________________________________________________________

______________________________________________________________

______________________________________________________________

- ☐ **Introduce caregiver to his role as coach during the phase of cue exposure. In addition, introduce how the toolbox and its tools can be used during the phase of cue exposure to manage strong emotions**

- ☐ **Check on Youth's Progress/Symptom Improvement with Caregiver**

Caregiver's view: ____________________________________________

______________________________________________________________

______________________________________________________________

______________________________________________________________

______________________________________________________________

______________________________________________________________

______________________________________________________________

______________________________________________________________

______________________________________________________________

______________________________________________________________

______________________________________________________________

______________________________________________________________

______________________________________________________________

______________________________________________________________

______________________________________________________________

Youth's view on his/her own progress: ____________________________________________

☐ Detail Progress Notes

# CHAPTER 9 Session 9: Approaching Cues

*This session should be conducted with the child.*

## MATERIALS NEEDED

- Thought/Body Feeling/Emotion/Behavior Square
- Thought/Body Feeling/Emotion/Behavior Square for Cues
- Worry/Anxiety Curve
- List of Potential Cues Worksheet
- Cue Response Chart
- Session 9 Review Form

## OUTLINE

- Process sessions 6 and 7 and assess the youth's grasp of progress.
- Evaluate the potential cues and, together with the child, identify a small set of cues (around three to five) to use in the exposure work.
- Educate the youth about cues' connection to thoughts, physiology, emotions, and behaviors.
- Introduce the Worry/Anxiety Curve and the goal of tolerating anxiety when responding to cues.

## Session Overview

### Goals

- Reinforce the child's acknowledgment of thoughts and feelings concerning her traumatic experiences.
- Identify cues jointly that will be used during the exposure.
- Prepare the youth for cue exposure by introducing the four components of every response:

1. **Emotional**: Examine three key emotions (fear, sadness, and anger)—*How you feel*
2. **Physical**: Examine arousal or detachment—*What you feel*
3. **Cognitive**: Examine positive and negative thoughts—*What and how you think*
4. **Behavioral**: Examine reaction—*What you do*

### Therapist's Role

- Identifying cues and introducing the Cue Response Chart
- Preparing the youth for the exposure sessions

## Processing of Sessions

During session 9, assess how the child processed the midtherapy session with the caregiver. The child may have reflections that she wants to share with you without the caregiver present. Reiterate the cognitive and emotional progress and reinforce the child's strengths. This conversation should include themes identified during sessions 6 and 7, which will lead to a discussion about cues.

## Evaluation of Cues

Review the List of Potential Cues Worksheet (Chapter 4, Worksheet 4.4) and get the child's feedback. The most important cues are those that ring true to the child—usually the ones the child offers herself.

There may be many cues and it may be impossible to work with all of them. Together with the child, identify three to five working cues for the exposure exercises. As the child learns about conditioning, she may become more attuned to specific cues. Relevant cues should be related intrinsically to both the traumatic history and the symptoms or maladaptive behaviors. Work with the Cue Response Chart (Worksheet 9.1) to illustrate visually the relationship between cues and the child's reactions.

### Cue Response Chart

Using the Cue Response Chart, identify thoughts, emotions, physical sensations, and behaviors—the four components associated with cues—that will be used during exposure. Explain that a reaction to a cue or a response is characterized by the four components, and to develop a new response, the child must change any one of these components. Brainstorm new ways of responding when exposed to cues.

### Establishment of Cues

A firm set of working cues should be established during this session. All potential cues should be considered. Ensure that working cues target the child's current behavioral and emotional problems. Including child's identified cues enhances her motivation and involvement in exposure. It also builds a sense of self-efficacy in the child.

### Reluctance toward Exposure

If the child is reluctant to engage in exposure, choose a low-threat cue to begin the work. Alternatively, you may choose to extend session 9 by an additional session.

### Difficulties in Identifying Cues

The child may also have difficulties identifying cues. Here is a script you can use to assist the child in identifying cues:

*When we talked about the bad things that happened, you told me you felt scared when you saw* [insert potential cue]. *How do you feel now when you see* [potential cue]*? What do you do when you see* [potential cue]*? How does your body feel when you see* [potential cue]*?*

You may also ask:

*Do you think any of the cues suggested by your caregiver trigger any of the problematic behaviors we have discussed?*

Remind the child that anything can be a cue. Some examples of cues from clinical scenarios include yelling, ambulance sirens, police cars, blood, needles, location where the traumas took place (e.g., street corner, tree in the backyard, former home, neighborhood park), belts, smell of smoke, loud noises (e.g., thunder), alcohol bottles, and the dark. Cues can be simple (e.g., colors, time of day), but can also be complex (e.g., relationships).

## Cues and the Thought/Body Feeling/Emotion/Behavior Square

Use the Thought/Body Feeling/Emotion/Behavior Square (originally included in Chapter 4, Worksheet 4.2, but duplicated here for your convenience [Worksheet 9.2]) to educate the youth about cue connections to thoughts, physiology, emotions, and behaviors. These four components are not only prompted by cues, but also they trigger each other. Therapy can profit from this association among components, when developing new responses. Working with only one of the corners of the Square can produce a change in the other three corners. Chapter 4 simply introduces the concept. Grasping the concept well is important before utilizing it here:

*We can start from any corner of the Square. Let's take the THOUGHT corner first. For example, you might say, "I remember when I got a bad grade" (which is a thought) and then you felt sad (which is an emotion). If you feel sad you may not want to go outside and play (which is a behavior) and you may feel tired (which is a body feeling). Changing the thought to "But I got a good grade yesterday" may start a whole new, more positive chain. Can you give me an example, starting with this corner?*

Continue giving examples starting with different corners, and each time ask the child for her own example. After the relationships among the corners of the Square are established, introduce the Thought/Body Feelings/Emotion/Behavior Square for Cues (Worksheet 9.3), which helps relate the responses to the cues. For some of the cues identified, illustrate how they can trigger the reactions in the square.

Clarify that these responses sometimes seem automatic, but it is important to pay attention to them. Explain to the child that if she is engaged in a reaction she does not like, she should then examine the square associated with that reaction.

Note that some children, according to their temperament, may be better suited to work with specific corners of the Square. An introspective, curious child may work better starting in the cognitive (thought) corner. An athlete who enjoys the relaxation exercises may prefer to start by doing mindfulness exercises to calm her perceived agitation (body feeling). A less psychologically minded child may just want to test new activities (behavior), whereas an emotionally attuned child may recognize the value of identifying and shifting her mood (emotion). Gaining insight into one's own temperament and preferred sequence helps the child manage the exposure exercises. It also helps the child in her ongoing work to achieve control over her reactions. The child's ability to understand responses and their relationship to cues is used later in therapy when developing new adaptive responses that will compete with current maladaptive responses.

## Responding to Cues: Worry/Anxiety Curve

The history of traumatic events has led to learned responses (e.g., anxiety, aggression) that may have been adaptive at one point or under certain scenarios. The Worry/Anxiety Curve (Worksheet 9.4) can facilitate the child's understanding of how having some anxiety may be appropriate, and that therapy targets the second half of the curve, where higher levels of anxiety disrupt function. Introduce the Worry/Anxiety Curve and demonstrate how the goal is not to eliminate worry or anxiety entirely, but to tolerate cues without becoming overly distressed.

**Worksheet 9.1**

## Cue Response Chart

*Instructions:* Write thoughts, emotions, physical sensations, and behaviors associated with cues.

| Cue | Thought | Body Feeling | Emotion | Behavior | Possible New Responses |
|---|---|---|---|---|---|
| | | | | | |

**Worksheet 9.2**

## Thought/Body Feeling/Emotion/Behavior Square

*Instructions:* Review how all reactions have four main components and how these influence each other.

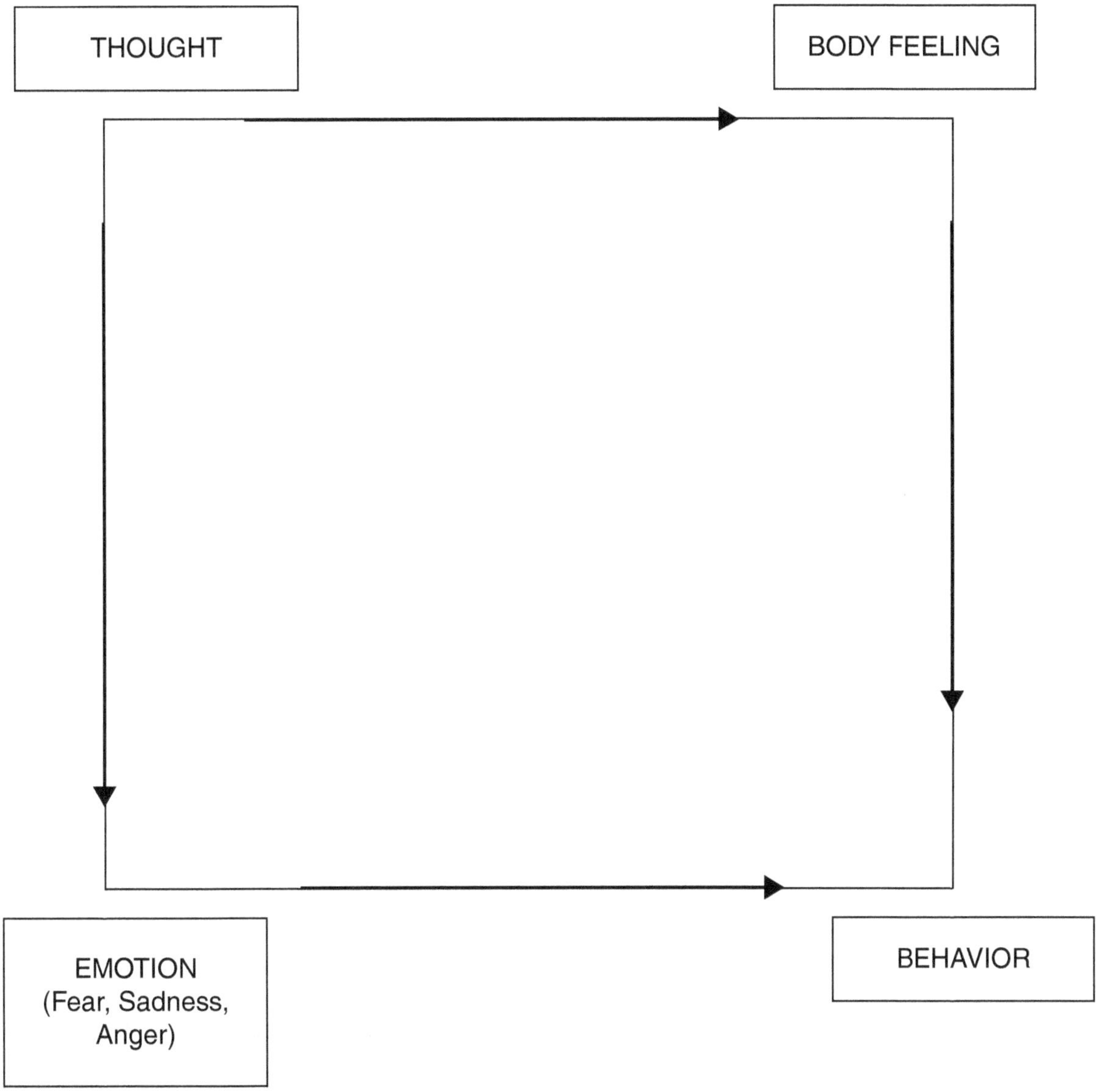

**Worksheet 9.3**

## Thought/Body Feeling/Emotion/Behavior Square for Cues

*Instructions:* Associate identified cues with their associated responses and their components.

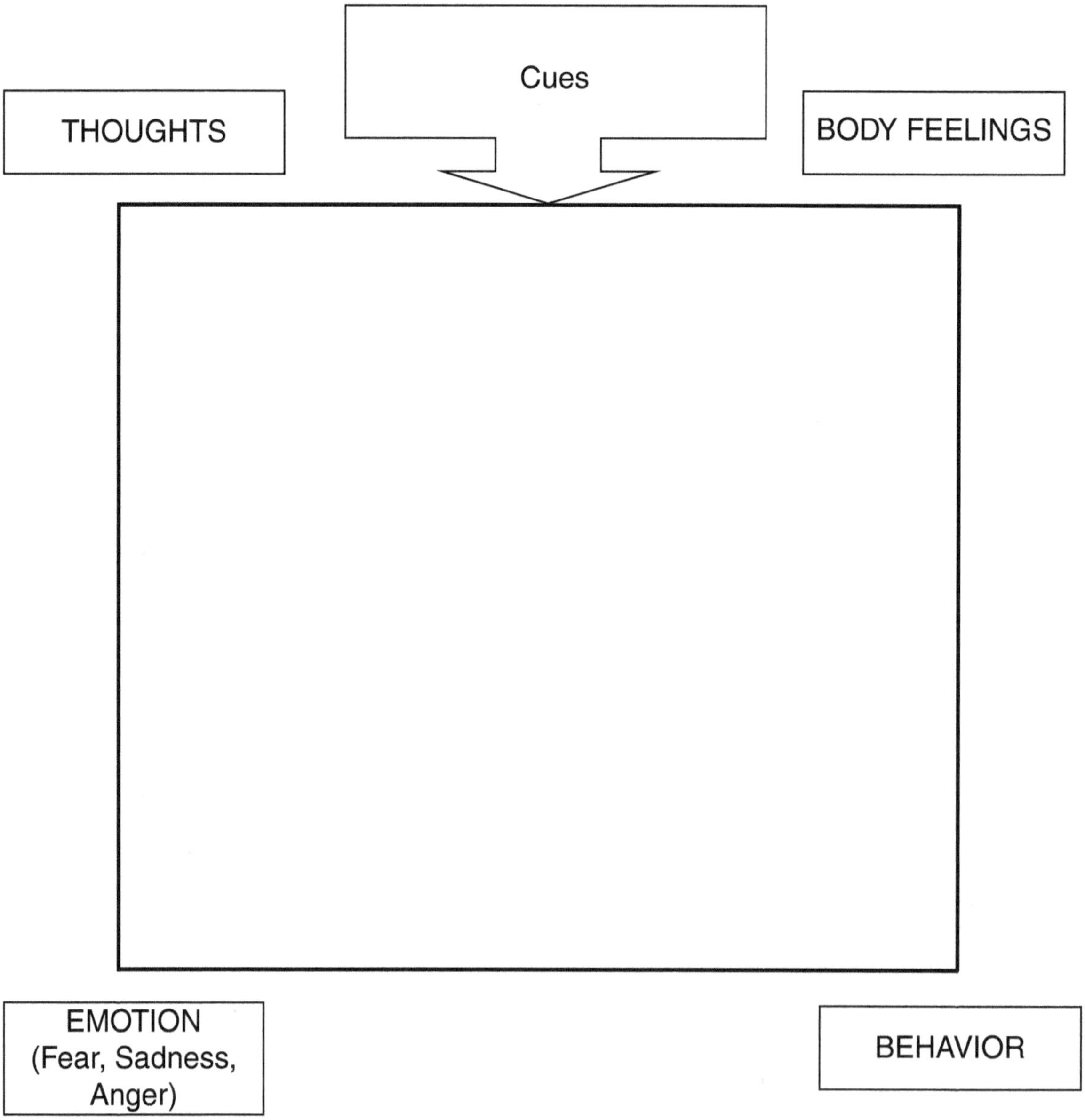

## Worry/Anxiety Curve

*Instructions: Illustrate the dynamic association between worry/anxiety and performance.*

Worry is not necessarily a bad thing. It can actually help you do better on activities (tests and sports, for example) up to a point. But, if you get too anxious, worry starts to become troublesome.

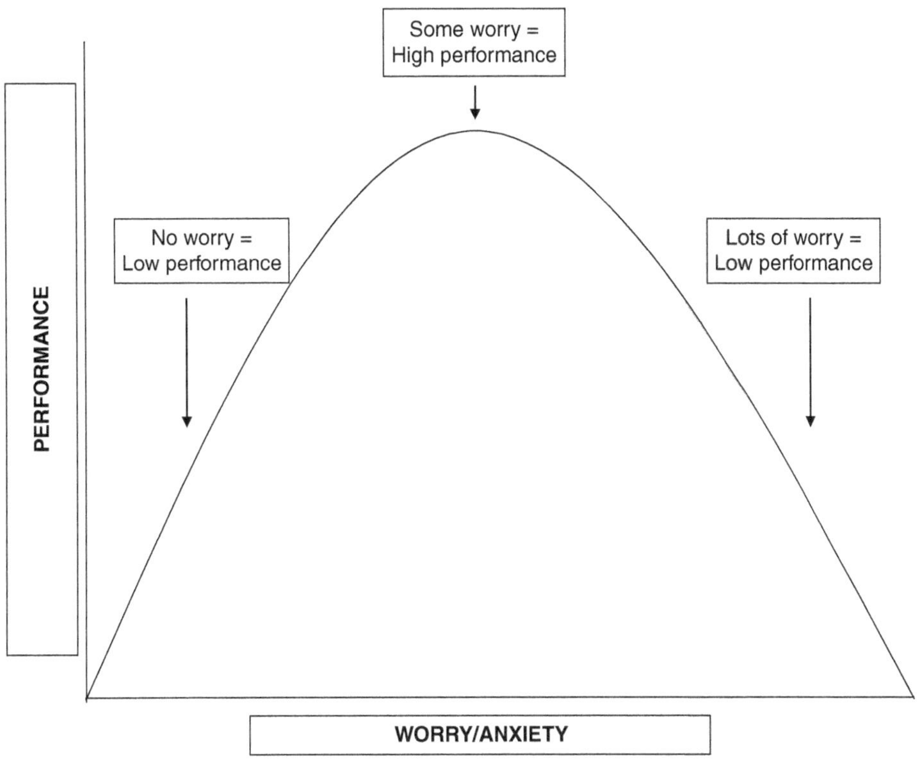

## Session 9 Review Form

*Instructions:* Please complete after session.

☐ **Check on Progress of Therapy with Youth**

☐ **Finalize Working Cues List (3–5) with Youth's Input**

Cues identified:

1.
2.
3.
4.
5.

☐ **Introduce the Thought/Body Feeling/Emotion/Behavior Square for Cues**

☐ **Identify Thought/Feeling/Emotion/Behavior Patterns**

☐ **Introduce the Cue Response Chart, Tying in the Square to Cues, and Have Youth Begin to Fill in the First Five Columns**

Cue-related patterns identified: ______________________________________________

______________________________________________________________________

______________________________________________________________________

______________________________________________________________________

☐ **Detail Progress Notes**

# CHAPTER 10 Session 10: Imaginary Exposure to Cues

*This session should be conducted with the child.*

## MATERIALS NEEDED

- Toolbox
- Cue Response Chart
- Thought/Body Feeling/Emotion/Behavior Square for Cues
- The Feelings Thermometer
- Session 10 Review Form

## OUTLINE

- Conduct in-session imaginary exposure to cues.
- Assist the child in developing new adaptive responses to cues.
- Proceed with gradual exposure as the child becomes comfortable with cues.

## Session Overview

Trauma-related symptoms are related to both the traumatic events and the stimuli associated with these fearful events. Symptoms and behavioral responses do not exist in a vacuum, but they may appear to be isolated or serendipitous when associations have not been recognized. In the following sessions we build on the insight gained in earlier sessions by doing exposure within a context the child understands. Experiencing cue-associated responses with a caring adult in the safety of a therapeutic session helps build tolerance to these cues. It also helps to disrupt the cycle between cue exposure and maladaptive response.

Early coupling between the traumatic events and temporally related stimuli (cues) are created at the time of the trauma. These associations are maintained and strengthened through subsequent avoidance strategies, which prevent new learning and new responses that challenge the misconception that neutral cues are threatening. Through exposure and insight, the child learns that cues are nonthreatening and that his responses to these cues can change.

Exposure weakens the association between traumatic cues and fear, helps extinguish the sensations of fear and threat, and allows for the formation of more adaptive responses. In this manner, exposure decreases the sensitized responsiveness to traumatic cues.

### Goal

- The youth continues to identify emotional, cognitive, behavioral, and physical responses that result from experiencing cues.

### Therapist's Role

- Teaching the application of Toolbox tools to responses identified in the Cue Response Chart
- Identifying the child's emotional state during exposure exercises and gauging his level using The Feelings Thermometer
- Applying tools from the Toolbox to advance exposure exercises as tolerated

## Imaginary Exposure to Cues

When confronted with cues, youth with posttraumatic symptoms tend to overinterpret their significance or catastrophize their presence. In this session, the child experiences no negative consequences when imagining the cues, although he witnesses his own response to these cues. This tactic allows the child an opportunity to gain insight into his disproportionate reaction to these otherwise neutral traumatic reminders. The Cue Response Chart (Chapter 9, Worksheet 9.1) can support this process by allowing the youth to examine the relationship between cues and current behaviors.

### Steps to In-Session Imaginary Exposure

1. Use a sample cue to illustrate how to use tools to manage the four components of its associated response.
2. Get a baseline rate of the child's emotional arousal using The Feelings Thermometer (Chapter 5, Worksheet 5.2).
3. Guide the child to imagine exposure to one of the cues from the List of Potential Cues (Chapter 4, Worksheet 4.4). Ask him to rate his level of distress using The Feelings Thermometer.
4. Use tools to lower the level of distress to baseline levels.
5. Amplify the magnitude of the cue or advance to a new cue as the child's emotional or physical reaction on exposure to the cue decreases.
6. Repeat this process for all working cues. If a cue is more salient than others, prioritize its practice.
7. Ask the child how his body and mind react to imagining the traumatic cues and add those details to the Cue Response Chart.

## Development of New Responses

Targeting current behaviors should not be the only approach during this session. There is some indication that learned couplings are difficult, if not impossible, to unlearn or extinguish. Therefore, in addition to weakening relationships between cues and responses, encourage the development of new responses with the Thought/Body Feeling/Emotion/Behavior Square for Cues (Chapter 9, Worksheet 9.4). New adaptive responses can be added to the Toolbox.

Concentrating only on extinguishing a specific maladaptive response can result in increased anxiety in the child and firmer adherence to this response. This may happen because this response may be the only tool the child has to manage his distress, and losing it may feel threatening. When competing, more adaptive responses are added to the Toolbox, the child will tend to choose responses that do not lead to conflict, and extinction of the maladaptive response may occur more naturally. Here is a case example:

*Mark has been able to decrease his emotional arousal to the sound of police sirens. Although he continues to scream when this happens, his response has been lessened. The therapist notices that the 9 rating in The Feelings Thermometer has decreased to a 5, but it does not seem to go any lower, and Mark is still distressed by his screaming response. Using the Thought/Body Feeling/Emotion/Behavior Square for Cues, Mark and the therapist are able to discuss that if his body feeling has changed ("I'm not as scared in my heart"), maybe the thought can change—for example, "The police must be attending to an important matter"—and then he may be able to have a competing response to screaming. Instead of screaming all the time, on one occasion he might ask his parents if something is happening in the neighborhood.*

## Gradual Exposure

Although "flooding" or implosive forms of exposure appear to have some utility in the treatment of anxiety disorders such as phobias or panic disorder, this form of treatment has seldom been applied in treating trauma in children. Inducing extreme fear in therapy may result in the child becoming overwhelmed and resorting to dysfunctional strategies, such as avoidance or dissociation. Youths' underdeveloped coping and emotional control strategies may make them particularly prone to becoming overwhelmed during exposure sessions. Therefore, most trauma exposure therapies use gradual exposure or systematic desensitization.

Gradual or systematic exposure, such as starting with imaginary exposure, involves a slow buildup of tolerance to distress. The therapist continually monitors the youth's emotional level using The Feelings Thermometer and encourages the use of tools to help control anxiety or other responses. During this session, the child first imagines trauma cues. In the next session and in take-home assignments, he is then exposed directly to trauma cues through role-play and "in vivo" exposure.

### Managing Anxiety during Cue Exposure

Cue exposure involves a balance between increasing anxiety to facilitate desensitization and containing anxiety to prevent the youth from shutting down. As the child grows comfortable with imagining a particular cue during session 10, raise the stakes either by increasing the magnitude of the imaginary cue (e.g., from a friend laughing to the whole classroom laughing to the whole school laughing loudly) and/or by moving on to a new cue. Here is a case example:

*Chelsea's house was flooded during Hurricane Katrina. Rain is identified as one of her cues. The therapist instructs Chelsea to imagine that it is raining. She begins to feel anxious, reporting her distress as a 4 on The Feelings Thermometer. The therapist encourages Chelsea to apply one of her tools—deep breathing—then repeats the imaginary exposure to rain. Using this tool helps Chelsea to decrease her anxiety level to a 2. The therapist then asks her to picture it raining as hard as it did in New Orleans when her house flooded. Chelsea becomes very anxious; this time, she reaches a 9 on the thermometer. She engages in deep breathing, as before, but also adds visual imagery. Chelsea states, "I am imagining that is raining in my special place, the special place is a safe, good place. Rain must be OK sometimes." By applying tools, Chelsea is eventually able to imagine the hurricane rain without feeling overwhelmed, and now has an anxiety level of 3.*

**Note:** There is no take-home activity after this session. The child has been introduced to exposure during this session and a negative experience at home may limit progress over the next sessions.

Worksheet 10.1

## Session 10 Review Form

*Instructions:* Please complete after session.

☐ **Determine Baseline Distress Level at beginning of Session Using The Feelings Thermometer (1–10)** ____________________________

☐ **Record Cues Imagined**

1. Cue: ______________________________________________________________________________

______________________________________________________________________________

______________________________________________________________________________

Initial distress level (1–10): __________ Concluding distress level (1–10): __________

Tools used: ______________________________________________________________________

______________________________________________________________________________

______________________________________________________________________________

Thoughts, body feelings, emotions, and behaviors identified during exposure: ____________

______________________________________________________________________________

______________________________________________________________________________

______________________________________________________________________________

______________________________________________________________________________

______________________________________________________________________________

______________________________________________________________________________

______________________________________________________________________________

2. Cue: ______________________________________________________________________________

______________________________________________________________________________

_______________________________________________

_______________________________________________

Initial distress level (1–10): __________ Concluding distress level (1–10): __________

Tools used: _______________________________________________

_______________________________________________

_______________________________________________

Thoughts, body feelings, emotions, and behaviors identified during exposure: ____________

_______________________________________________

_______________________________________________

_______________________________________________

_______________________________________________

_______________________________________________

_______________________________________________

_______________________________________________

3. Cue: _______________________________________________

_______________________________________________

_______________________________________________

_______________________________________________

Initial distress level (1–10): __________ Concluding distress level (1–10): __________

Tools used: _______________________________________________

_______________________________________________

_______________________________________________

_______________________________________________

Thoughts, body feelings, emotions, and behaviors identified during exposure: ____________

_______________________________________________________________________________

_______________________________________________________________________________

_______________________________________________________________________________

_______________________________________________________________________________

_______________________________________________________________________________

_______________________________________________________________________________

_______________________________________________________________________________

☐ **Detail Progress Notes**

# CHAPTER 11 Session 11: In-Session Exposure to Cues

*This session should be conducted with the child.*

## MATERIALS NEEDED

- Cue Response Chart
- The Feelings Thermometer
- Toolbox
- Thought/Body Feeling/Emotion/Behavior Square for Cues
- Feelings Worksheets
- Session 11 Review Form

## OUTLINE

- Using cues from session 10, role-play with youth situations in which trauma cues elicit anxiety and other trauma-related thoughts, body feelings, emotions or behaviors.
- Practice using tools in the Toolbox during the role-play situations.
- Using the responses and emotions identified in the Feelings Worksheets, tie these worksheets to the Cue Response Chart. This exercise links traumatic history, cues, and responses.
- Assign the youth in vivo exposure to cues as a take-home activity.

## Session Overview

Session 11 continues the systematic exposure process that began during session 10. In this session, the cues are experienced more directly. Rather than thinking about rain, for example, the child and therapist may make the sound of rain or listen to water from an open faucet.

For this process to build up tolerance effectively, the cues must be consistent, with session 11 involving the same cues as those emphasized during session 10. It is not necessary to address every identified cue during these sessions. The goal is to teach strategies for managing cues. Gained insight and self-efficacy may facilitate generalization to other cues and situations.

### Goal

- The youth manages emotional, cognitive, behavioral, and physical responses that result from experiencing cues.

### Therapist's Role

- Teaching the application of Toolbox tools to items identified in the Cue Response Chart by exposing the child to cues through role-playing and simulation
- Being empathic about earlier responses the child might have developed in attempts to manage distress

## Role-Play of Scenarios with Cues

During this session, the therapist and child role-play scenarios that involve traumatic cues (select from the same cues imagined during session 10). These scenarios do not involve a recreation of the traumatic events. Instead, the role-play is focused on the inherently neutral cues. Cues' negative valence arises only from their association with the traumatic history. The role-play should involve reacting to cues in the present rather than at the time of the trauma. This prepares the child for the next session, in which real-life exposure is addressed. If the caregiver is engaged as a coach, a take-home activity will be assigned. In this activity the child, with the caregiver's support, is exposed to a cue and the caregiver notes the child's response. Together, the therapist and the child will choose a cue that is tolerable and that has been useful in previous sessions for the in vivo exposure.

**Instructions for Role-Play**

1. Choose a cue that has been imagined during session 10 for further exposure with role-play.
2. Get a baseline rate of emotional arousal using The Feelings Thermometer. Similarly, use the thermometer during role-play or simulation, and during and after the application of tools.
3. Role-play a scenario that includes the cue. The scenario should be a present-day one, not a recreation of the traumatic event.
4. Encourage practice of tools for managing distress during role-play.
5. Identify thoughts, body feelings, emotions, and behaviors during the exposure and add youth's self-observations to the Cue Response Chart (Chapter 9, Worksheet 9.1).
6. Identify potential new adaptive responses.

Record the role-play/simulation of cues on the Session 11 Review Form (Worksheet 11.1).

## Practice of Tools during Role-Play Situations

As in session 10, sessions 11 and 12 provide opportunities for reinforcing previously acquired skills (practice of tools) and solidifying insight regarding the three key emotions (fear, sadness, and anger) and the four components of a reaction or response (thought, body feeling, emotion, and behavior). Throughout exposure, encourage the child to use the tools she has learned to manage her distress or symptoms (Toolbox, Chapter 4, Worksheet 4.3). Practicing tools within the safety of the therapeutic environment leads to better management of cues in real-life situations. Although the child may not always be able to identify the trigger that sets her off, she can nevertheless identify her own distress and recruit appropriate tools.

During the imaginary and in-session exposure sessions, query the youth continually regarding her current cognitions, emotions, and physiological responses. This serves to model self-awareness and provides a concrete application of the Thought/Body Feeling/Emotion/Behavior Square for Cues (Chapter 9, Worksheet 9.3). The youth's self-observations can be added to the Cue Response Chart (Chapter 9, Worksheet 9.1), enhancing the youth's understanding of her unique response pattern. Revisiting these forms and the Feelings worksheets (Chapter 6, Worksheets 6.2–6.4) emphasizes the etiology of the youth's problem behaviors, places these behaviors in the context of the history, and eliminates negative self-attributions associated with the problematic behaviors. Understanding this sequence can provide relief from trauma symptoms. Here is a case example:

*Shane experienced physical abuse by his stepfather, and witnessed domestic violence between the stepfather and his mother. His stepfather's voice frequently grew loud before he became violent. Shane identified loud voices as one of his cues. As a role-play, the therapist exposed Shane to a loud voice after telling him she would do that. The therapist asked loudly, "Where did I put my keys?" After this, the therapist checked on Shane's distress level, and asked him what he thought and felt during the role-play. Shane reported that he thought that maybe he had lost the keys, that he felt scared, and that his body felt shaky.*

During this session, it is important to reiterate that the youth's current state (emotional, cognitive, physiological, and/or behavioral) is reasonable and normal given what she has experienced. The traumatic event resulted in certain feelings and thoughts, which continue to influence the youth's behaviors. According to the Thought/Body Feeling/Emotion/Behavior Square for Cues (Chapter 9, Worksheet 9.3), all these components influence each other. Remind the child that cues can trigger any component of the Square, setting off a response cycle. And, changing one component of the Square can result in an entirely new pattern and a more adaptive response.

The main objective of exploring the response pattern to cues is to create behavioral change. Your empathy should address any self-blame for the traumatic history and current behavioral problems. This fundamental understanding from the therapist is essential if the youth is to develop new, more adaptive responses.

As the child receives positive feedback on her work during the in-session exposure, she gains self-efficacy. This benefits the outcome of future exposures, such as the take-home activity.

## Take-Home Activities

✐ Assign exposure to the working cues as tolerated at home. Recruit the caretaker to coach the exposure, track the responses, and note which coping tools were used.

**Worksheet 11.1**

## Session 11 Review Form

*Instructions:* Please complete after session.

☐ **Determine Baseline Distress Level at beginning of Session Using The Feelings Thermometer (1–10) ________**

☐ **Describe Role-Play/Simulation of Cues**

1. Cue: ______________________________________________

______________________________________________

______________________________________________

Initial distress level (1–10): ________ Concluding distress level (1–10): ________

Tools used: ______________________________________________

______________________________________________

______________________________________________

Thoughts, body feelings, emotions, and behaviors identified during exposure: __________

______________________________________________

______________________________________________

______________________________________________

______________________________________________

______________________________________________

______________________________________________

Current response to cue: ______________________________________________

______________________________________________

______________________________________________

Potential new adaptive response to cue: ____________________

2. Cue: ____________________

Initial distress level (1–10): __________ Concluding distress level (1–10): __________

Tools used: ____________________

Thoughts, body feelings, emotions, and behaviors identified during exposure: ____________

Current response to cue: ______

Potential new adaptive response to cue: ______

3. Cue: ______

Initial distress level (1–10): ______ Concluding distress level (1–10): ______

Tools used: ______

Thoughts, body feelings, emotions, and behaviors identified during exposure: ____________

____________________________________________________________

____________________________________________________________

____________________________________________________________

____________________________________________________________

____________________________________________________________

____________________________________________________________

Current response to cue: ______________________________________

____________________________________________________________

____________________________________________________________

____________________________________________________________

____________________________________________________________

____________________________________________________________

____________________________________________________________

Potential new adaptive response to cue: ____________________________

____________________________________________________________

____________________________________________________________

____________________________________________________________

____________________________________________________________

____________________________________________________________

____________________________________________________________

☐ **Detail Progress Notes**

# CHAPTER 12 Session 12: Evaluation of In-Vivo Exposure Assignment

*This session should be conducted with the child.*

## MATERIALS NEEDED

- Toolbox
- Cue Response Chart
- Thought/Body Feeling/Emotion/Behavior Square for Cues
- Life Timeline
- Session 12 Review Form

## OUTLINE

- Review exposure assignments and solve problems with tool roadblocks.
- Update the Cue Response Chart with any new information gained during the exposure assignments.
- Remind the child that there are only three sessions left and talk about what will happen during those sessions.

## Session Overview

During the previous two sessions, the child was exposed to cues that often caused distress, posttraumatic symptoms, and behavioral problems. The Toolbox (Chapter 4, Worksheet 4.3) and The Feelings

Thermometer (Chapter 5, Worksheet 5.2) were used to facilitate the exposure and tolerate the cues. Cognitive coupling of cues with traumatic history may persist, but the child now recognizes the role of cues in his responses.

The gradual exposure provides the child with control and contains the overwhelming affect that may result from confronting traumatic material. Maintaining anxiety and distress at tolerable levels prevents reliance on avoidance or disengagement strategies that could interfere with therapeutic progress. Addressing increasingly more challenging cues sequentially and practicing coping tools contributes to the youth's sense of self-efficacy.

The in vivo exposure assignment is the peak of the hierarchy of fears that the youth confronts during this phase of therapy. The sense of mastery acquired during the imaginary and in-session exposures facilitates adherence to an in vivo home assignment. Although this exposure may seem premature, it foreshadows the upcoming closing sessions, after which the child will continue to be exposed to cues.

Session 12 is devoted primarily to evaluating the in vivo exposure, with a particular focus on the utility of tools in responding to traumatic cues. The Thought/Body Feeling/Emotion/Behavior Square for Cues (Chapter 9, Worksheet 9.3) helps identify and make concrete the association of these components of an original response, and helps facilitate the development of more adaptive responses.

### Goal

- Assist the youth in developing a new repertoire of responses to traumatic cues.

### Therapist's Role

- Identifying roadblocks to using the Toolbox
- Identifying any new tools the child may have developed during the exercise
- Introducing the upcoming closing sessions

## Review of Exposure Assignments and Tool Development

Discuss the in vivo homework assignment and any problems the child had with the application of the Toolbox, as well as any new tools he developed. Add any new tools to the Toolbox.

Note any roadblocks to using the tools during this in vivo assignment (Worksheet 12.1). Then, collaborate with the youth to find ways to alter or adapt the tools to increase their effectiveness, and brainstorm how these or other tools can be used in future situations. Some tools may be particularly useful, but only during specific scenarios or with specific cues. Identifying these patterns should help the utility of the Toolbox. Here is a case example:

*Eduardo experienced success with using deep breathing both during therapy and at home. However, he shared with the therapist that he felt anxious that he might draw attention to himself if he were to use this tool in class. The therapist works with Eduardo to practice breathing more unobtrusively and also reminds him of other tools he could use in class, such as positive thought insertion or asking his teacher for a break.*

## Update of Cue Response Chart

The real-world experience provides an opportunity to reevaluate the Cue Response Chart (Chapter 9, Worksheet 9.1), expanding on the youth's description of his response pattern and as facilitated by the Thought/Body Feeling/Emotion/Behavior Square for Cues (Chapter 9, Worksheet 9.3).

## Preparation for Closing Sessions

Termination of therapy can be a difficult time for youths with a history of trauma. Termination may act as a cue to prior experiences associated with disrupted attachment, abandonment, or trust. These issues should be anticipated prior to the closing sessions. The life timeline (Chapter 6, Worksheet 6.1), the traumatic history of the child, and his narrative should inform you on how to prepare for the closing sessions. Using a term such as *graduation* may help a child compare this experience with other academic transitions he has experienced and may facilitate the termination process.

To ameliorate any distress associated with termination, the impending graduation is first discussed during session 12. Work with the child on preparing for this transition. Termination itself should be construed as an opportunity to learn about the cue response association and also to address any reasonable feelings associated with ending therapy.

## Worksheet 12.1

# Session 12 Review Form

*Instructions*: Please complete after session.

☐ **Evaluate the in Vivo Assignment** ______________________________

______________________________

______________________________

______________________________

______________________________

☐ **Identify Any New Tools from the Assignment** ______________________________

______________________________

______________________________

______________________________

______________________________

☐ **Identify Tool Roadblocks**

1. Roadblock: ______________________________

______________________________

______________________________

Potential solution(s): ______________________________

______________________________

______________________________

2. Roadblock: ______________________________

______________________________

______________________________

Potential solution(s): ____________________________________________

____________________________________________

____________________________________________

3. Roadblock: ____________________________________________

____________________________________________

____________________________________________

Potential solution(s): ____________________________________________

____________________________________________

____________________________________________

☐ **Remind Youth of Upcoming Graduation from Therapy and Summarize the Activities of the Next Three Sessions**

## ☐ Detail Progress Notes

## ✓ PHASE 4

# CHAPTER 13 Session 13: Processing Chronic Traumatic Stress History

*This session should be conducted with the child.*

## MATERIALS NEEDED

- Session 13 Review Form
- Life Timeline

## OUTLINE

- Encourage the youth to retell her traumatic stress history, incorporating information learned during the sessions.
- Assess acknowledgment of emotions, cognitions, and physical and behavioral reactions as the youth relates the story of her life.

## Session Overview

Posttraumatic symptoms are maintained through a variety of factors. The traumatic events activate a reflexive fear response; ongoing traumatic events reinforce these networks and eventually they generalize to become activated by trauma-related cues, current stressors, and current emotional states. The avoidance of trauma-related cues and their associated emotional and physiological responses results in the maintenance of response patterns even if they become maladaptive. Avoidance prevents the development of appropriate responses for trauma-related cues.

In session 13, the youth applies her newly acquired insight into her chronic traumatic stress history, and approaches and verbalizes a narrative that is informed by her work in therapy. This process allows the therapist to evaluate the youth's progress and areas that need focused attention after therapy. During the closing session with the caregiver, the therapist makes any needed recommendations for further evaluation or treatment.

### Goal

- The child expresses how she survived the negative events of her life, and discusses her emotions and thoughts about all adverse events. The youth and the therapist highlight strengths in the child that have allowed for resilience after these events.

### Therapist's Role

- Evaluating the youth's progress in therapy
- Assessing the preservation of a realistic, nonself-blaming narrative
- Providing empathy and positive reinforcement on the work completed by the child

## Retelling of Traumatic Stress History

Ask the youth to retell her traumatic stress history, incorporating information learned during the sessions and as facilitated by the work completed with the life timeline (Chapter 6, Worksheet 6.1). The child and the therapist may wish to edit or update this form based on the work done during therapy. The child should be encouraged to discuss the impact of the traumatic events in her life, and identify and label body feelings and emotions associated with cues for those events. The new adaptive responses should bring a brighter outlook to the narrative.

## Assessment of New Narrative

During sessions 4 and 5, the traumatic history was explored with the life timeline. During sessions 6 and 7, the chronic traumatic stress history was processed with the child and cognitive distortions were corrected. This session is used to assess the stability of that work:

- Has the child incorporated lessons learned into her story?
- Does the story verbalize previously unexpressed events, emotions, or body feelings?
- How are the present exposure to cues and new adaptive responses to cues integrated into her story?

The new narrative should not be a sanitized version of the child's history. It should not discredit her experience of the events. The objective is to correct any guilt or shame-based distortions that do not allow the child to move forward in her healing. In our work, we find guilt to be a strong predictor in the development of posttraumatic symptoms. The new narrative should be realistic, should be integrated into the rest of her life, should reflect empowerment and self-efficacy, and should be informed by her response to cues and her new management strategies. Use the Session 13 Review Form (Worksheet 13.1) to record information from the new narrative and to document the child's progress in therapy.

**Worksheet 13.1**

## Session 13 Review Form

*Instructions*: Please complete after session.

☐ **Record Corrected Themes on Chronic Traumatic Stress History** ____________________

☐ **List Corrected Attributions** ____________________

☐ **Label Emotions**

☐ **Evaluate Youth's Therapy Progress**

☐ **Detail Progress Notes**

# CHAPTER 14 Session 14: Closing Session 1

*This session should be conducted with the youth and the caregiver.*

## MATERIALS NEEDED

- Session 14 Review Form
- Natural Course of Clinical Improvement handout

**Note**: The therapist should complete the Session 14 Review Form (Worksheet 14.1) before this session begins to have information available for the caregiver.

## OUTLINE

- Review the child's progress in therapy.
- Make recommendations for future treatment.
- Educate about the nature of clinical improvement.

### Session Overview

Up to this point, the caregivers' participation has been limited to three sessions only and their potential involvement as coach during the in vivo exposure. More involvement from caregivers is always positive, but we acknowledge the difficulties of engaging caregivers who also experience ongoing adversity. Session 14 allows the therapist to offer a description of the treatment process with an appreciation for the work done by the child and as supported by the caregiver. In addition, it offers a realistic view on what to expect and recommendations for future steps.

### Goal

- Provide the caregiver with final clinical observations, results of treatment, and recommendations.

### Therapist's Role

- Discussing clinical progress
- Discussing the potential need for treatment of comorbid conditions or future posttraumatic symptom reoccurrences

## Review of Progress

During this first closing session, meet with the child and caregiver to do the following:

- Present the child's strengths and how they facilitated the therapeutic work. This provides an opportunity to bolster the child's self-esteem, value his contribution, and model to the parent the significance of highlighting strengths.
- Identify progress, challenges, and roadblocks to clinical progress.

These important factors will probably continue to play a role in the child's life and it is imperative to acknowledge them and offer recommendations that are based on these factors.

## Recommendations for Future Treatment

When making recommendations for future treatment, take the child's progress and current challenges into account, provide recommendations as indicated on the session 14 Review Form, identify residual symptoms and conditions, and suggest next treatment approaches.

Provide education about the role of prevention and the noncontinuous nature of clinical improvement, as illustrated on the Natural Course of Clinical Improvement handout (Worksheet 14.2). Highlight how, even at the lower points of progress, the clinical picture is not as it was at the beginning point. In addition, this worksheet illustrates that the path to improvement is not a straight line; rather, it is characterized by highs and lows.

Although caregiver involvement in the treatment may have been limited, the caregiver's role in the child's life is not. Next steps need to include the caregiver as a facilitator of the ongoing work. In other words, the caregiver must be encouraged to remind the child of the work done in treatment, and how to use the tools learned and knowledge gained during treatment.

## Session 14 Review Form

*Instructions: Prepare this form before meeting with the caregiver and revise it as necessary after the meeting.*

### ☐ Present List of Child's Strengths

______________________ ______________________

______________________ ______________________

______________________ ______________________

### ☐ Present Recommendations and Rationale

Choose as needed

- ☐ Individual therapy   Referred to: ______________________
- ☐ Once per month
- ☐ Once every 3 months
- ☐ Once every 6 months
- ☐ Once a week
- ☐ Every two weeks

Recommend if indicated

- ☐ Family therapy
- ☐ Caregivers' couples therapy
- ☐ Individual therapy for other family members

Based on residual symptoms or other conditions, recommend if indicated

- ☐ Medication evaluation
- ☐ Psychological testing
- ☐ Individualized Education Plan meeting

### ☐ Identify Residual Symptoms and Other Conditions

______________________________________________

______________________________________________

☐ Discuss Progress in Therapy and Roadblocks to Progress, If Applicable

☐ Educate on the Role of Prevention and the Nonlinear Nature of Improvement (Use Clinical Improvement Graph on Natural Course Of Clinical Improvement Handout)

☐ **Detail Progress Notes**

## Natural Course of Clinical Improvement

*Instructions: Please share with caregiver and child as you discuss the natural course of clinical improvement.*

The natural course of clinical improvement is not a straight line. The graph shown here depicts how, after some therapeutic gains, it is normal to return to earlier behaviors. The overall trajectory of treatment, however, needs to be noted. If therapeutic gains are occurring, this return to maladaptive behaviors is not as severe or as long-lasting as it may have been in the past.

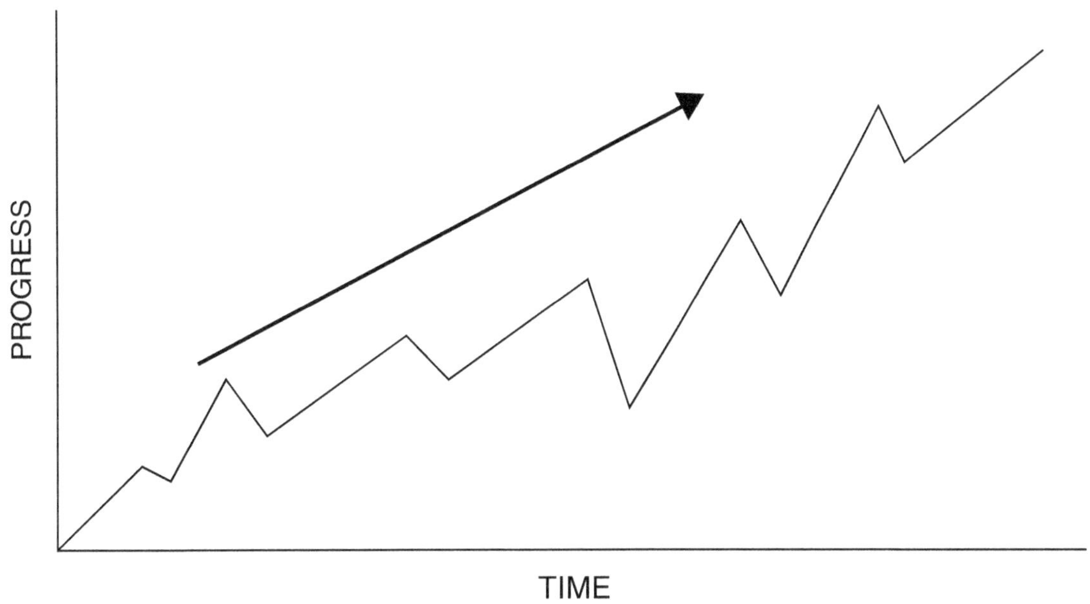

# CHAPTER 15 Session 15: Closing Session 2

*This session should be conducted with the youth.*

## MATERIALS NEEDED

- Toolbox
- Session 15 Review Form

## OUTLINE

- If in your work during this treatment you have used standardized assessments, be prepared to give the final wave in this session.
- Process session 14 with the child.
- Brainstorm potential future uses of tools and model tool application.
- Encourage and answer questions as therapy comes to an end.

### Session Overview

By design, there is one more meeting with the child only to underscore the active role the child has played in her recovery. The session allows time for addressing any ongoing questions she may have and for the therapist to give any final recommendations as needed. There needs to be an acknowledgment of the continuing nature of the work, even after the end of therapy.

### Goals

- Provide the child positive feedback on work done in therapy.
- Solve potential problems with child on how to confront future challenges.

### Therapist's Role

- Reviewing therapeutic gains
- Educating about how to retain gains and how to get help if needed in the future

## Review of Standardized Assessments

In your individual practice or if conducting research, you may choose to monitor progress with behavioral, cognitive, or other instruments. You may report these results to the child during this session (assuming scoring is complete).

## Processing of Session 14

The child will probably have thoughts about the previous meeting with the caregiver (session 14). Encourage her to share them or ask questions about anything that was not clear. Inquire about your role during this session and the child's role. You may also want to ask the child about her expectations for the future and provide realistic hope based on your experience with her during treatment.

## Future Tool Application

Identify with the child those elements in the different tools that have been particularly beneficial. Discuss with her how to make these part of her daily routine and how to integrate them into her strengths armamentarium.

Discuss with the child her thoughts on the utility and benefits of this treatment experience. Ask her how this experience affects her wish or desire to engage in such work later in her life, if needed. Thank her for being a partner with you during this process.

## Session 15 Review Form

*Instructions*: Please complete after session.

☐ **Review Youth's Strengths and Progress**

☐ **Brainstorm New Applications for Tools**

☐ **Answer Any Remaining Questions**

☐ **Provide a Posttherapy Structured Youth Assessment, If Used during Earlier Sessions**

☐ Detail Progress Notes

# References

Abram, K. M., Teplin, L. A., Charles, D. R., Longworth, S. L., McClelland, G. M., & Dulcan, M. K. (2004). Posttraumatic stress disorder and trauma in youth in juvenile detention. *Archives of General Psychiatry, 61*(4), 403–410.

Abram, K., Washburn, J., Teplin, L., Emanuel, K., Romero, E., & McClelland, G. (2007). Posttraumatic stress disorder and psychiatric comorbidity among detained youths. *Psychiatric Services, 58*(10), 1311–1316.

Amaya-Jackson, L., Reynolds, V., Murray, M. C., McCarthy, G., Nelson, A., Cherney, M. S., et al. (2003). Cognitive–behavioral treatment for pediatric posttraumatic stress disorder: Protocol and application in school and community settings. *Cognitive and Behavioral Practice, 10*(3), 204–213.

American Psychiatric Association. (2013). *Diagnostic and statistical manual of mental disorders* (5th ed.). Washington, DC: Author.

Anda, R. F., Felitti, V. J., Bremner, J. D., Walker, J. D., Whitfield, C., Perry, B. D., et al. (2006). The enduring effects of abuse and related adverse experiences in childhood. *European Archives of Psychiatry and Clinical Neuroscience, 256*(3), 174–186.

Beck, A. (1976). *Cognitive therapy and the emotional disorders.* New York: International Universities Press.

Bedard-Gilligan, M., & Zoellner, L. A. (2012). Dissociation and memory fragmentation in post-traumatic stress disorder: An evaluation of the dissociative encoding hypothesis. *Memory, 20*(3), 277–299.

Bendall, S., Alvarez-Jimenez, M., Hulbert, C. A., McGorry, P. D., & Jackson, H. J. (2012). Childhood trauma increases the risk of post-traumatic stress disorder in response to first-episode psychosis. *Australian and New Zealand Journal of Psychiatry, 46*(1), 35–39.

Bower, G. H., & Sivers, H. (1998). Cognitive impact of traumatic events. *Development and Psychopathology, 10*(04), 625–653.

Brewin, C. R., & Holmes, E. A. (2003). Psychological theories of posttraumatic stress disorder. *Clinical Psychology Review, 23*(3), 339–376.

Brewin, C. R., & Saunders, J. (2001). The effect of dissociation at encoding on intrusive memories for a stressful film. *British Journal of Medical Psychology, 74*(4), 467–472.

Briere, J., Kaltman, S., & Green, B. L. (2008). Accumulated childhood trauma and symptom complexity. *Journal of Traumatic Stress, 21*(2), 223–226.

Brosky, B. A., & Lally, S. J. (2004). Prevalence of trauma, PTSD, and dissociation in court-referred adolescents. *Journal of Interpersonal Violence, 19*(7), 801–814.

Buckner, J. C., Beardslee, W. R., & Bassuk, E. L. (2004). Exposure to violence and low-income children's mental health: Direct, moderated, and mediated relations. *American Journal of Orthopsychiatry, 74*(4), 413–423.

Carrey, N. J., Butter, H. J., Persinger, M. A., & Bialik, R. J. (1995). Physiological and cognitive correlates of child abuse. *Journal of the American Academy of Child & Adolescent Psychiatry, 34*(8), 1067–1075.

Carrion, V. G., Kletter, H., Weems, C. F., Berry, R. R., & Rettger, J. P. (2013). Cue-centered treatment for youth exposed to interpersonal violence: A randomized controlled trial. *Journal of Traumatic Stress, 26*(6), 654–662.

Carrion, V. G., Weems, C. F., Ray, R. D., Glaser, B., Hessl, D., & Reiss, A. L. (2002a). Diurnal salivary cortisol in pediatric posttraumatic stress disorder. *Biological Psychiatry, 51*(7), 575–582.

Carrion, V. G., Weems, C. F., Ray, R., & Reiss, A. L. (2002b). Toward an empirical definition of pediatric PTSD: The phenomenology of PTSD symptoms in youth. *Journal of the American Academy of Child & Adolescent Psychiatry, 41*(2), 166–173.

Chaffin, M., & Friedrich, B. (2004). Evidence-based treatments in child abuse and neglect. *Children and Youth Services Review, 26*(11), 1097–1113.

Chemtob, C. M., Nakashima, J., & Carlson, J. G. (2002a). Brief treatment for elementary school children with disaster-related posttraumatic stress disorder: A field study. *Journal of Clinical Psychology, 58*(1), 99–112.

Chemtob, C. M., Nakashima, J. P., & Hamada, R. S. (2002b). Psychosocial intervention for postdisaster trauma symptoms in elementary school children: A controlled community field study. *Archives of Pediatrics & Adolescent Medicine, 156*(3), 211–216.

Chu, D. A., Williams, L. M., Harris, A. W., Bryant, R. A., & Gatt, J. M. (2013). Early life trauma predicts self-reported levels of depressive and anxiety symptoms in nonclinical community adults: Relative contributions of early life stressor types and adult trauma exposure. *Journal of Psychiatric Research, 47*(1), 23–32.

Cisler, J. M., Begle, A. M., Amstadter, A. B., Resnick, H. S., Danielson, C. K., Saunders, et al. (2012). Exposure to interpersonal violence and risk for PTSD, depression, delinquency, and binge drinking among adolescents: Data from the NSA-R. *Journal of Traumatic Stress, 25*(1), 33–40.

Cloitre, M., Chase Stovall-McClough, K., Miranda, R., & Chemtob, C. M. (2004). Therapeutic alliance, negative mood regulation, and treatment outcome in child abuse-related posttraumatic stress disorder. *Journal of Consulting and Clinical Psychology, 72*(3), 411–416.

Cloitre, M., Koenen, K. C., Cohen, L. R., & Han, H. (2002). Skills training in affective and interpersonal regulation followed by exposure: A phase-based treatment for PTSD related to childhood abuse. *Journal of Consulting and Clinical Psychology, 70*(5), 1067–1074.

Cohen, J. A. (1998). Practice parameters for the assessment and treatment of children and adolescents with posttraumatic stress disorder. *Journal of the American Academy of Child & Adolescent Psychiatry, 37*(10 Supplement), 4S–26S.

Cohen, J. A., Berliner, L., & Mannarino, A. (2010). Trauma focused CBT for children with co-occurring trauma and behavior problems. *Child Abuse & Neglect, 34*(4), 215–224.

Cohen, J. A., Deblinger, E., Mannarino, A. P., & Steer, R. A. (2004). A multisite, randomized controlled trial for children with sexual abuse-related PTSD symptoms. *Journal of the American Academy of Child & Adolescent Psychiatry, 43*(4), 393–402.

Cohen, J. A., & Mannarino, A. P. (2000). Predictors of treatment outcome in sexually abused children. *Child Abuse & Neglect, 24*(7), 983–994.

Cohen, J. A., & Mannarino, A. P. (2008). Trauma-focused cognitive behavioural therapy for children and parents. *Child and Adolescent Mental Health, 13*(4), 158–162.

Cohen, J. A., Mannarino, A. P., Berliner, L., & Deblinger, E. (2000). Trauma-focused cognitive behavioral therapy for children and adolescents: An empirical update. *Journal of Interpersonal Violence, 15*(11), 1202–1223.

Cohen, J. A., Mannarino, A. P., & Iyengar, S. (2011a). Community treatment of posttraumatic stress disorder for children exposed to intimate partner violence: A randomized controlled trial. *Archives of Pediatrics & Adolescent Medicine, 165*(1), 16–21.

Cohen, J. A., Mannarino, A. P., Kliethermes, M., & Murray, L. A. (2012). Trauma-focused CBT for youth with complex trauma. *Child Abuse & Neglect, 36*(6), 528–541.

Cohen, J. A., Mannarino, A. P., & Knudsen, K. (2005). Treating sexually abused children: 1 Year follow-up of a randomized controlled trial. *Child Abuse & Neglect, 29*(2), 135–145.

Cohen, J. A., Mannarino, A. P., & Murray, L. K. (2011b). Trauma-focused CBT for youth who experience ongoing traumas. *Child Abuse & Neglect, 35*(8), 637–646.

Cohen, J. A., Mannarino, A. P., Perel, J. M., & Staron, V. (2007). A pilot randomized controlled trial of combined trauma-focused CBT and sertraline for childhood PTSD symptoms. *Journal of the American Academy of Child & Adolescent Psychiatry, 46*(7), 811–819.

Cohen, J. A., Perel, J. M., DeBellis, M. D., Friedman, M. J., & Putnam, F. W. (2002). Treating traumatized children: Clinical implications of the psychobiology of posttraumatic stress disorder. *Trauma, Violence, & Abuse, 3*(2), 91–108.

Cooley-Strickland, M., Quille, T. J., Griffin, R. S., Stuart, E. A., Bradshaw, C. P., & Furr-Holden, D. (2009). Community violence and youth: Affect, behavior, substance use, and academics. *Clinical Child and Family Psychology Review, 12*(2), 127–156.

Copeland, W. E., Keeler, G., Angold, A., & Costello, E. J. (2007). Traumatic events and posttraumatic stress in childhood. *Archives of General Psychiatry, 64*(5), 577–584.

Costello, E. J., Erkanli, A., Fairbank, J. A., & Angold, A. (2002). The prevalence of potentially traumatic events in childhood and adolescence. *Journal of Traumatic Stress, 15*(2), 99–112.

Cuffe, S. P., Addy, C. L., Garrison, C. Z., Waller, J. L., Jackson, K. L., McKeown, R. E., et al. (1998). Prevalence of PTSD in a community sample of older adolescents. *Journal of the American Academy of Child & Adolescent Psychiatry, 37*(2), 147–154.

Dalgleish, T. (2004). Cognitive approaches to posttraumatic stress disorder: The evolution of multirepresentational theorizing. *Psychological Bulletin, 130*(2), 228–260.

Daviss, W. B., Mooney, D., Racusin, R., Ford, J. D., Fleischer, A., & McHugo, G. J. (2000). Predicting posttraumatic stress after hospitalization for pediatric injury. *Journal of the American Academy of Child & Adolescent Psychiatry, 39*(5), 576–583.

Deblinger, E., McLeer, S. V., & Henry, D. (1990). Cognitive behavioral treatment for sexually abused children suffering post-traumatic stress: Preliminary findings. *Journal of the American Academy of Child & Adolescent Psychiatry, 29*(5), 747–752.

Deblinger, E., Stauffer, L. B., & Steer, R. A. (2001). Comparative efficacies of supportive and cognitive behavioral group therapies for young children who have been sexually abused and their nonoffending mothers. *Child Maltreatment, 6*(4), 332–343.

de Kloet, C., Vermetten, E., Geuze, E., Kavelaars, A., Heijnen, C., & Westenberg, H. (2006). Assessment of HPA-axis function in posttraumatic stress disorder: Pharmacological and non-pharmacological challenge tests: A review. *Journal of Psychiatric Research, 40*(6), 550–567.

Donnelly, C. L., & Amaya-Jackson, L. (2002). Post-traumatic stress disorder in children and adolescents. *Pediatric Drugs, 4*(3), 159–170.

Dorsey, S., Briggs, E. C., & Woods, B. A. (2011). Cognitive–behavioral treatment for posttraumatic stress disorder in children and adolescents. *Child and Adolescent Psychiatric Clinics of North America, 20*(2), 255–269.

Dunmore, E., Clark, D. M., & Ehlers, A. (2001). A prospective investigation of the role of cognitive factors in persistent posttraumatic stress disorder (PTSD) after physical or sexual assault. *Behaviour Research and Therapy, 39*(9), 1063–1084.

Dyregrov, A., & Yule, W. (2006). A review of PTSD in children. *Child and Adolescent Mental Health, 11*(4), 176–184.

Ehlers, A., & Clark, D. M. (2000). A cognitive model of posttraumatic stress disorder. *Behaviour Research and Therapy, 38*(4), 319–345.

Ehlers, A., Mayou, R., & Bryant, B. (2003). Cognitive predictors of posttraumatic stress disorder in children: Results of a prospective longitudinal study. *Behaviour Research and Therapy, 41*(1), 1–10.

Ellis, B. H., Fogler, J., Hansen, S., Forbes, P., Navalta, C. P., & Saxe, G. (2012). Trauma systems therapy: 15-Month outcomes and the importance of effecting environmental change. *Psychological Trauma: Theory, Research, Practice, and Policy, 4*(6), 624–631.

Elsesser, K., Sartory, G., & Tackenberg, A. (2004). Attention, heart rate, and startle response during exposure to trauma-relevant pictures: A comparison of recent trauma victims and patients with posttraumatic stress disorder. *Journal of Abnormal Psychology, 113*(2), 289–301.

Fani, N., Tone, E. B., Phifer, J., Norrholm, S. D., Bradley, B., Ressler, K. J., et al. (2012). Attention bias toward threat is associated with exaggerated fear expression and impaired extinction in PTSD. *Psychological Medicine, 42*(3), 533–543.

Farrell, S. P., Hains, A. A., & Davies, W. (1998). Cognitive behavioral interventions for sexually abused children exhibiting PTSD symptomatology. *Behavior Therapy, 29*(2), 241–255.

Feeny, N. C., Foa, E. B., Treadwell, K. R., & March, J. (2004). Posttraumatic stress disorder in youth: A critical review of the cognitive and behavioral treatment outcome literature. *Professional Psychology: Research and Practice, 35*(5), 466–476.

Finkelhor, D., Turner, H., Ormrod, R., & Hamby, S. L. (2010). Trends in childhood violence and abuse exposure: Evidence from 2 national surveys. *Archives of Pediatrics & Adolescent Medicine, 164*(3), 238–242.

Ghosh Ippen, C., Harris, W. W., Van Horn, P., & Lieberman, A. F. (2011). Traumatic and stressful events in early childhood: Can treatment help those at highest risk? *Child Abuse & Neglect, 35*(7), 504–513.

Grasso, D. J., Joselow, B., Marquez, Y., & Webb, C. (2011). Trauma-focused cognitive behavioral therapy of a child with posttraumatic stress disorder. *Psychotherapy, 48*(2), 188–197.

Hansen, R., Gaynes, B., Thieda, P., Gartlehner, G., Deveaugh-Geiss, A., Krebs, E., et al. (2008). Meta-analysis of major depressive disorder relapse and recurrence with second-generation antidepressants. *Psychiatric Services, 59*(10), 1121–1130.

House, A. S. (2006). Increasing the usability of cognitive processing therapy for survivors of child sexual abuse. *Journal of Child Sexual Abuse, 15*(1), 87–103.

Inslicht, S. S., Metzler, T. J., Garcia, N. M., Pineles, S. L., Milad, M. R., Orr, S. P., et al. (2013). Sex differences in fear conditioning in posttraumatic stress disorder. *Journal of Psychiatric Research, 47*(1), 64–71.

Kessler, R. C., Berglund, P., Demler, O., Jin, R., Merikangas, K. R., & Walters, E. E. (2005). Lifetime prevalence and age-of-onset distributions of DSM-IV disorders in the National Comorbidity Survey Replication. *Archives of General Psychiatry, 62*(6), 593–602.

Kilpatrick, D. G., Ruggiero, K. J., Acierno, R., Saunders, B. E., Resnick, H. S., & Best, C. L. (2003). Violence and risk of PTSD, major depression, substance abuse/dependence, and comorbidity: Results from the National Survey of Adolescents. *Journal of Consulting and Clinical Psychology, 71*(4), 692–700.

King, N. J., Tonge, B. J., Mullen, P., Myerson, N., Heyne, D., Rollings, S., et al. (2000). Treating sexually abused children with posttraumatic stress symptoms: A randomized clinical trial. *Journal of the American Academy of Child & Adolescent Psychiatry, 39*(11), 1347–1355.

Kletter, H., Weems, C. F., & Carrion, V. G. (2009). Guilt and posttraumatic stress symptoms in child victims of interpersonal violence. *Clinical Child Psychology and Psychiatry, 14*(1), 71–83.

Langley, A. K., Nadeem, E., Kataoka, S. H., Stein, B. D., & Jaycox, L. H. (2010). Evidence-based mental health programs in schools: Barriers and facilitators of successful implementation. *School Mental Health, 2*(3), 105–113.

Lansford, J. E., Dodge, K. A., Pettit, G. S., Bates, J. E., Crozier, J., & Kaplow, J. (2002). A 12-year prospective study of the long-term effects of early child physical maltreatment on psychological, behavioral, and academic problems in adolescence. *Archives of Pediatrics & Adolescent Medicine, 156*(8), 824–830.

Lewis, T., Thompson, R., Kotch, J. B., Proctor, L. J., Litrownik, A. J., English, D. J., et al. (2012). Parent–youth discordance about youth-witnessed violence: Associations with trauma symptoms and service use in an at-risk sample. *Child Abuse & Neglect, 36*(11–12), 790–797.

Many, M. M. (2009). Termination as a therapeutic intervention when treating children who have experienced multiple losses. *Infant Mental Health Journal, 30*(1), 23–39.

March, J. S., Amaya-Jackson, L., Murray, M. C., & Schulte, A. (1998). Cognitive–behavioral psychotherapy for children and adolescents with posttraumatic stress disorder after a single-incident stressor. *Journal of the American Academy of Child & Adolescent Psychiatry, 37*(6), 585–593.

Mendenhall, A. N., Fristad, M. A., & Early, T. J. (2009). Factors influencing service utilization and mood symptom severity in children with mood disorders: Effects of multifamily psychoeducation groups (MFPGs). *Journal of Consulting and Clinical Psychology, 77*(3), 463–473.

Merikangas, K. R., He, J.-P., Burstein, M., Swanson, S. A., Avenevoli, S., Cui, L., et al. (2010). Lifetime prevalence of mental disorders in US adolescents: Results from the National Comorbidity Survey Replication–Adolescent Supplement (NCS-A). *Journal of the American Academy of Child & Adolescent Psychiatry, 49*(10), 980–989.

Mowrer, O. (1960). *Learning theory and behavior.* New York: Wiley.

National Institute of Mental Health. (2013). *Helping children and adolescents cope with violence and disasters: What parents can do.* NIH publication no. 13-3518. Bethesda, MD: US Government Printing Office.

Newman, C. L., & Motta, R. W. (2007). The effects of aerobic exercise on childhood PTSD, anxiety, and depression. *International Journal of Emergency Mental Health, 9*(2), 133–158.

Nikulina, V., Widom, C. S., & Czaja, S. (2011). The role of childhood neglect and childhood poverty in predicting mental health, academic achievement and crime in adulthood. *American Journal of Community Psychology, 48*(3–4), 309–321.

Overbeek, M., de Schipper, J., Lamers-Winkelman, F., & Schuengel, C. (2012). The effectiveness of a trauma-focused psycho-educational secondary prevention program for children exposed to interparental violence: Study protocol for a randomized controlled trial. *Trials, 13*(1), 1–13.

Perrin, S., Smith, P., & Yule, W. (2000). Practitioner review: The assessment and treatment of post-traumatic stress disorder in children and adolescents. *Journal of Child Psychology and Psychiatry, 41*(3), 277–289.

Plattner, B., Silvermann, M. A., Redlich, A. D., Carrion, V. G., Feucht, M., Friedrich, M. H., et al. (2003). Pathways to dissociation: Intrafamilial versus extrafamilial trauma in juvenile delinquents. *The Journal of Nervous and Mental Disease, 191*(12), 781–788.

Pollak, S., Cicchetti, D., & Klorman, R. (1998). Stress, memory, and emotion: Developmental considerations from the study of child maltreatment. *Development and Psychopathology, 10*(04), 811–828.

Rodgers, C. S., Lang, A. J., Laffaye, C., Satz, L. E., Dresselhaus, T. R., & Stein, M. B. (2004). The impact of individual forms of childhood maltreatment on health behavior. *Child Abuse & Neglect, 28*(5), 575–586.

Ruf, M., Schauer, M., Neuner, F., Catani, C., Schauer, E., & Elbert, T. (2010). Narrative exposure therapy for 7-to 16-year-olds: a randomized controlled trial with traumatized refugee children. *Journal of Traumatic Stress, 23*(4), 437–445.

Rust, J. O., & Troupe, P. A. (1991). Relationships of treatment of child sexual abuse with school achievement and self-concept. *The Journal of Early Adolescence, 11*(4), 420–429.

Saltzman, K. M., Weems, C. F., & Carrion, V. G. (2006). IQ and posttraumatic stress symptoms in children exposed to interpersonal violence. *Child Psychiatry and Human Development, 36*(3), 261–272.

Scheeringa, M. S., Weems, C. F., Cohen, J. A., Amaya-Jackson, L., & Guthrie, D. (2011). Trauma-focused cognitive–behavioral therapy for posttraumatic stress disorder in three- through six-year-old children: A randomized clinical trial. *Journal of Child Psychology and Psychiatry, 52*(8), 853–860.

Scheeringa, M., Zeanah, C., & Cohen, J. (2010). PTSD in children and adolescents: Toward an empirically based algorithm. *Depression & Anxiety*, 28, 1–13.

Schneider, S. J., Grilli, S. F., & Schneider, J. R. (2013). Evidence-based treatments for traumatized children and adolescents. *Current Psychiatry Reports, 15*(1), 1–9.

Shipman, K. L., & Zeman, J. (2001). Socialization of children's emotion regulation in mother–child dyads: A developmental psychopathology perspective. *Development and Psychopathology, 13*(2), 317–336.

Silva, R. R., Alpert, M., Munoz, D. M., Singh, S., Matzner, F., & Dummit, S. (2000). Stress and vulnerability to posttraumatic stress disorder in children and adolescents. *American Journal of Psychiatry, 157*(8), 1229–1235.

Silva, R. R., Cloitre, M., Davis, L., Levitt, J., Gomez, S., Ngai, I., et al. (2003). Early intervention with traumatized children. *Psychiatric Quarterly, 74*(4), 333–347.

Silverman, W. K., Ortiz, C. D., Viswesvaran, C., Burns, B. J., Kolko, D. J., Putnam, F. W., et al. (2008). Evidence-based psychosocial treatments for children and adolescents exposed to traumatic events. *Journal of Clinical Child & Adolescent Psychology, 37*(1), 156–183.

Smith, P., Perrin, S., Dalgleish, T., Meiser-Stedman, R., Clark, D. M., & Yule, W. (2013). Treatment of posttraumatic stress disorder in children and adolescents. *Current Opinion in Psychiatry, 26*(1), 66–72.

Terranova, A. M., Boxer, P., & Morris, A. S. (2009). Factors influencing the course of posttraumatic stress following a natural disaster: Children's reactions to Hurricane Katrina. *Journal of Applied Developmental Psychology, 30*(3), 344–355.

Trowell, J., Kolvin, I., Weeramanthri, T., Sadowski, H., Berelowitz, M., Glasser, D., et al. (2002). Psychotherapy for sexually abused girls: Psychopathological outcome findings and patterns of change. *The British Journal of Psychiatry*, *180*(3), 234–247.

Wagner, A. P. (2002). *Worried no more: Help and hope for anxious children*. Rochester, NY: Lighthouse Press.

Widom, C. S., Czaja, S. J., & Dutton, M. A. (2008). Childhood victimization and lifetime revictimization. *Child Abuse & Neglect*, *32*(8), 785–796.

# About the Author

**Victor G. Carrión, MD,** is a professor of psychiatry and behavioral sciences, and director of the Stanford Early Life Stress and Pediatric Anxiety Program at Stanford University. He is also Chair of the California Mental Health Services Oversight and Accountability Commission. Dr. Carrión received his doctoral degree at Mount Sinai School of Medicine and completed his psychiatry residency at the University of Pennsylvania. He completed fellowship training in child and adolescent psychiatry, normal development, and developmental trauma at Stanford University. For the past 20 years Dr. Carrión has studied the biological, psychological, and social ramifications of early life stress and has worked to develop systems of care that address this major public health issue.

# Epilogue

## MAYA'S SONG

*I know why the caged bird sings*
*and still I hold the dream*
*I came here to help them find*
*the light within the soul.*
*I did not come for money*
*and I did not come for fame*
*I did not come, even for love*
*but I did not come to fear.*
*I came here for freedom*
*and to set the caged bird free.*
*to set the caged bird free.*

*Let's stop fighting for freedom*
*and find another way*
*think of all the children*
*and the ones still on the way*
*All the money spent on fighting*
*could heal the entire world*
*Let mothers teach their children*
*that guns are not the way*
*never the way.*

*I came here for freedom*
*and to set the caged bird free.*
*Martin and Maya and Mandela too*
*they held the dream for you*
*let not their lives go by in vain*
*lets end the senseless pain*
*Stop hurting one another*
*and bring back the dream*

*I know why the caged bird sings*
*and still I hold the dream*
*I came here for freedom*
*and to set the caged bird free*
*to set the caged bird free.*

Music and lyrics by Lynn Flory, copyright 2015; Craftsbury Common, Vermont. Published here with permission from the author. With acknowledgment to *I Know Why the Caged Bird Sings* by Maya Angelou.

www.ingramcontent.com/pod-product-compliance
Lightning Source LLC
Chambersburg PA
CBHW062150131025
33986CB00021B/639
*9780190201326*